Don & CJ
Thanks for all the
Jerry West

AN EAGLE'S EYE VIEW

TERRY WILLMAN

An Eagle's Eye View.
Copyright © 2001 by Terry Willman. All Rights Reserved.
Printed in the United States of America.
No part of this book may be used or reproduced in any manner whatsoever without written permission, except in the case of brief quotations embodied in critical articles or reviews.

For information, address Terry Willman
P.O. Box 54895
Phoenix, Arizona 85078-4895

Published by: Terry and Karie Willman
Visit our site at: www.aneagleseyeview.net

Edited by: Clinton Willman

Cover Designs and Graphics:
Rhonda Hitchcock Cre8tvshop
Email: Cre8tvshop@earthlink.net

ISBN 0-929690-57-5

First Printing: October, 2001

Acknowledgements

Without the help and contribution of the following, this story would never have been told.

First, I'd like to thank my wife, Karie and our two daughters Jennifer and Rachael, for their complete support; Clinton Willman for his editing and grammar; Dan Shea for supplying me with pictures and maps of South Vietnam and to help fill in the blanks on some of those days; Gene Parks for his insight and recollection on particular incidents that happened; Bill Griffith for hunting down technical data included in my book; Reggie Kenner for his insights; Roger Olsson for his slides of Nam while we were there and also for his recollection of certain events that took place; Don Hodges for his continuous help; Betsy O'Reilly for her professional expertise; and David Mussey and Gary Whitty, without their efforts and website Lancer Home Page: http://members.tripod.com/dmussey/, I would have never known about the 658's restoration.

My special thanks to Marshall Trimble, Arizona's Official State Historian.

Thanks to all for making this book possible!

–Terry Willman

Forward

In July of 2000 I received the quarterly newsletter that two of my fellow Lancers, David Mussey and Gary Whitty, publish. Contained in this newsletter was an article from the 101st Airborne Association newsletter. Someone wanted information on the UH-1H S/N 67-17658 which saw service with the B Company 101st Aviation Battalion in Vietnam during 1968-69. They wanted any information on an accident involving this aircraft at Fire Base Eagle's Nest on May 31, 1969. It had been over thirty years since I was in Vietnam, but the number rang a bell. I took out the journal I kept in Vietnam and it was my old helicopter.

I called the gentleman listed in the article and told him I was the Crew Chief on 658. I then told him about the crash. He said they had a lot of information from the co-pilot and door gunner. He was trying to locate the pilot. I asked him why he wanted all the information; he told me he was with the Firelands Military Museum in Ohio, and they had restored 658 (you may view it at http://www.huey.org). He also said they took it to parades and other functions, and it had even been parked at the Vietnam War Memorial in Washington, D.C. Hearing this, it brought tears to my eyes. I was proud to hear that my old friend had suddenly come back to life. I decided then that since I knew its history from August of 1968 to May of 1969, I could provide more detail than just the one day that it had crashed.

When I actually started writing, some days I became very angry when remembering certain events. I kept at it, not to let my feelings stop what I hoped would be a worthy project. My main goal is to generate enough interest in the 658 so it will be part of our country's history. The 658 is probably one of the very few helicopters whose entire history in a combat zone is known, especially on a day-to-day basis.

Introduction

An Eagle's Eye View is a day-by-day account of tail number 67-17658 one of many Bell UH-1H helicopters assigned to Vietnam. I was its only Crew Chief during our training in Colorado and while combating enemy forces in South Vietnam; therefore, my story must also be told in conjunction with 658. This historical text is strictly that, historical. I make no fanciful elaborations as to what went on over there, nor do I try to theorize the war or its political agenda. Most of the information contained herein came directly from my journal, which I kept during my tour of duty. I used letters I wrote home which fortunately, were kept by my family; and recollections from some of my friends to assist me in adding more detail to certain days.

In a sense, this text is a reproduction of that journal, outlining in great detail 658's role in the U.S. Army and my experiences with it. This text rarely deviates from this formula, except to clarify certain points or to add personal remarks when necessary. I start from the beginning, with my orders to report to Fort Carson, Colorado in July of 1968, and continue up until the time 658 crashed on Fire Support Base Eagle's Nest on 31 May 1969.

Writing my story in this way, I hope to give the reader an opportunity to experience and understand what flying in a combat zone was like and the hardships endured while in South Vietnam. These hardships not only include the tension, anxiety and excitement felt on a combat assault mission, but also the grind of everyday life while just trying to survive such things as the food and weather in Vietnam.

Now, some of you might ask what is a crew chief? As Crew Chief I was responsible for all the working components on the UH-1H, making sure that they were safe for flight. If something on the aircraft required repairs, I resolved the problem. I either fixed the helicopter on the flight line or sent it to the hanger so that the heavy maintenance section of our outfit could repair it. I determined 658's airworthiness and whether or not it flew. After every single mission, be it combat or anything else, I performed the post-flight inspection of the aircraft, cleaning or fixing whatever needed repair. I was extremely meticulous in these duties, for my life and the lives of my other crewmembers were at stake.

I have included at the end of my book the general information and scope section from the Military manual for the UH-1H: Aircraft Preventive Maintenance Daily Inspection checklist. This is to give an overall view of what duties were performed at the end of each day or prior to the next day's flight. This manual is a later version of the one we actually had in Vietnam but basically covers the same inspections.

My duties, however, did not stop on the flight line but continued while in the air. During a mission, I constantly assessed the status of our aircraft's systems, and I kept a watchful eye on the instruments in order to determine if we took any damage after a hot landing zone. The amount of weight we could safely carry was another one of my responsibilities.

This criteria had many factors, including air temperature, altitude, weather, and amount of fuel. The most critical aspect of my flight duties pertained to the main and tail rotor blades. When entering or leaving a landing zone, I surveyed the area, making sure the aircraft would clear any obstacles. At times, I helped guide the pilots into particularly difficult landing zones. As an added bonus, I sat behind an M-60 machine gun, which made me a prime target for the enemy.

Before I continue with my story, I must take this opportunity to make one thing perfectly clear. Being the Crew Chief or Door Gunner on a UH-1H helicopter was strictly voluntary. The Army did not assign us those particular positions, and whoever wanted to "quit" and go work in maintenance could do so. However, there were incentives to being a part of a helicopter crew: you never pulled guard duty, succumbed to being a part of the kitchen police or had to serve on outhouse detail!

An Eagle's Eye View

In July of 1968, I received orders to report to Fort Carson, Colorado. The unit being formed was the 158th Assault Helicopter Battalion and I was assigned to B Company. Alpha, Bravo and Charlie Companies were UH-1H transport companies and Delta Company was our gunship company. There were a total of sixty UH-1H helicopters and twenty Cobra gunships. All of our helicopters came right from the factory in August of 1968, and I was assigned tail number 67-17658. I had not seen a helicopter since February of 1968 when I completed the single rotor turbine utility repairman school at Fort Eustis, Virginia. The training we received in school was extensive. We learned about the turbine engine and all of its working components. The fuel system is complex with filters you have to check and clean.

On aircraft, especially helicopters, vibrations are so strong that it loosens the bolts and screws. To prevent the hardware from becoming loose, holes are drilled through the heads of the bolts and screws and then wired in such a way that if one starts to loosen it automatically tightens the bolts or screws and vice versa. This configuration keeps everything tight but makes working on them time consuming. We also had to learn how the electrical system worked and what functions governed what operation. We studied the hydraulic system, which controlled the rotor system and in turn, determined your direction of flight. We learned about the main pylon system, which also controlled our direction of flight, and the tail rotor system, which counteracted the torque of the main rotor blades. This was critical because without it you would spin like a top with no control. It wasn't like working on my old '56 Chevy.

After completing my training at Fort Eustis, my new MOS (military occupational service) designation was 67 N 20. I was now a qualified Crew Chief for a UH-1H helicopter. I then received orders to report to the 5th Mechanized Division at Fort Hood, Texas. I spent six months at Fort Hood practicing riot control, and on field maneuvers I drove our platoon leader, a 2nd Lieutenant, around in a jeep. This sucked because many nights I slept fully clothed in combat gear because we were on a twenty-minute standby to be sent to anywhere in the United States to quell the civil rights riots our country was going through during that period of time. Because of this assignment, I was happy to see orders sending me to an aviation unit.

A week after my arrival at Fort Carson, they selected twenty of us as crew chiefs for our company. We also learned that we were going to be attached to the 3rd Brigade 101st Airborne Division in South Vietnam. Their unit insignia is the American Bald Eagle, and the nickname for the outfit is the "Screaming Eagles," hence the title of my book, *An Eagle's Eye View*. Since I had not seen a helicopter in six months, I found all of the repair manuals for the UH-1H and started reading and refreshing my memory.

Our pilots were fresh from flight school. We called them "wobbly ones." They were mostly warrant officers who received their officer's commissions after completing flight school. The first crew of 658 was WO1-Ed Sakenes, WO1-Dan Shea, and myself, SP4-Terry Willman. I didn't know then that of all the pilots I ever flew with, these two would be two of the best.

Our first flight was on 3 September 1968, and we flew a total of five hours that day. Our battalion commander had our pilots practice flying different combat formations. They were also practicing takeoffs and landings on different types of terrain. I just sat in the back watching the gauges on the console panel, and I also kept an eye on how close our main rotor blades were to the ship next to us when we were flying in tight formations. We only logged another 12.8 hours in September, all devoted to training flights. The best part was that Dan and Ed decided to teach me how to fly. Their reasoning made sense to me. If they both should get shot, they wanted me to be able to get them back to camp. I did not do too badly, and I could actually hover and hold it fairly steady after a few of their lessons.

Mike Doris, Butts Army Airfield FT. Carson, Colorado

UH-1H Flying in Formation

During September, the Army worked us from dawn to dusk. Three of the days I spent qualifying with the M-16, M-60 machine gun, .38 caliber Smith & Wesson revolver, .45 caliber Colt model M-1911A1, and the M-79 grenade launcher, which would all be used later. Also during this month we all had to go through an escape and evasion course. Mike Dorris and I were the first to make it to the final checkpoint. Our 1st Sergeant was so happy we were from his company he gave us a three day pass. When Mike and I got back from our leave, we heard that they were still looking for guys that were lost in the mountains.

In October of 1968 we started flying more in the mountains around Colorado Springs practicing contour flying. We flew one resupply mission to a company of Green Berets that were camped on the top of Cheyenne Mountain. On 14 October 1968,

An Eagle's Eye View

Butts Army Airfield, Fort Carson, Colorado

we flew cross-country to Oklahoma City, Oklahoma, allowing the pilots to practice long distance navigation. From 24 to 27 October our unit spent four days in the field. We flew to the gunnery range and practiced live fire exercises, simulating combat situations. These missions took place both day and night. Flying low level at 100 knots is really something. We logged 48.2 hours of flight time in October.

In November of 1968 we continued practicing field maneuvers and spent seven more days out in the field. Colorado was cold and had about two feet of snow on the ground. Great training for Vietnam? We flew a total of 33.9 hours.

My last flight stateside at Fort Carson in Colorado Springs was 4 December 1968, and we flew for one hour. At this time some of our pilots and maintenance personnel were unfortunately selected to fly all of our company aircraft to Sharp Army

Airfield in California. Our aircraft were then transported to the Oakland Naval Yard where they were prepared for shipment aboard a naval vessel to South Vietnam. The main rotors and tail rotors had to be taken off all of the aircraft for transport aboard the naval vessel. During this time most of the crew chiefs and other company personnel were sent home on leave because there was not much for us to do. I was one of the lucky ones, since I could spend Christmas with my family before being shipped off to South Vietnam. Our departure date from Colorado Springs was set for 19 February 1969.

In February, prior to our departure, we were issued all of our jungle fatigues and combat equipment, including our M-16's. The Army made arrangements with Northwest Orient Airlines for several planes to transport us to South Vietnam. On 19 February 1969, dressed in our combat fatigues and carrying our M-16s, we boarded our commercial flights in Colorado Springs. I remember it was snowing when we left. Our first stop was Seattle, Washington to refuel. From there, we flew to Anchorage, Alaska, also to refuel. Somehow, a ladies club in Alaska had heard that a whole aviation unit was coming through on commercial flights and they were there at two o'clock in the morning serving us coffee and donuts. I will never forget those ladies and I want to take the opportunity here to thank them again. When we left Anchorage it was snowing hard. We flew overseas to Japan and I could not believe it was snowing in Japan too!

After we left Japan for the last leg of our flight, the plane became really quiet. I was sitting on the plane with two of my closest friends, Roger Olsson and Gene Parks. We were all wondering what we had gotten ourselves into. The other thing on our minds was how we would react when people started shooting at us. We would find out soon enough.

An Eagle's Eye View

Here is where my journal begins:
21 February 69: When I stepped off the plane in Da Nang, South Vietnam it was like stepping into an oven. The 100-degree plus temperature and 90-percent humidity was a shock to the body. In minutes we were all drenched in sweat. We had arrived in Vietnam near the tail end of their monsoon season. We had to wait out on the runway for them to unload our duffle bags from the plane. I felt like I was going to melt away. When we finally gathered up our gear, we headed for some shade. Each of us personally carried his military 201 file, and we had to process in country. After processing, we went back out to the airfield to wait for a C-130 (air force transport plane) to take us to our next stop, Hue Phu Bai. The C-130's were made to take off and land in a short distance. When we were loaded up and they brought the engines up to full power, the plane sounded like everything inside was loose and ready to fall apart. The takeoff, flight, and landing on this C-130 was like riding on a roller coaster. From Hue Phu Bai we were going to be taken to Camp Evans on CH-47's (chinook army transport helicopter). While waiting for our next ride, we had our first meal in South Vietnam C-Rations. The one thing you did not have to worry about here was heating your meals. They were already pre-heated. When we were loading onto the CH-47's the door gunners sitting behind their machine guns were the first thing you noticed. This is when I realized I was actually in a war zone. Our flight to Camp Evans was at 500 feet and as fast as that CH-47 could go. On this flight I had my first good look at the countryside. There were numerous rice patties with dikes surrounding them and little villages scattered around. We were flying along the main high-

way route (Highway 1) traveling north. When I saw Camp Evans from the air, it did not look impressive. It seemed small and was sort of an oblong shape with barbwire and bunkers surrounding its perimeter. When we landed at Camp Evans, I thought to myself "what a hellhole."

Battalion sent some of the personnel from each company to Camp Evans prior to our arrival to set up things. They had a crude airfield-landing pad and places to park our helicopters when they arrived from the states. They had tents set up for us to live in temporarily until The Sea Bees (naval construction crews) could come and build our permanent hooches. The first thing they had us do after storing our gear in the tents was fill sandbags to start building bunkers. Everyone pitched in doing this, even the officers. We worked on this detail all day in 116-degree heat. When it started to rain late in the afternoon, it helped cool us off, and we worked until dark. Our CO (company commander) told us that after working all day, drinking hours were from five to seven o'clock, but they would only allow you two cans of beer. You could not get drunk if you tried. We then started hearing the perimeter bunker guards firing their M-79 grenade launchers to discourage Charlie (the enemy) from coming in. Later on that night, the siren went off, which meant we were getting hit. We grabbed our weapons and started heading for our bunkers. We heard some explosions in the distance and that was it. The all-clear signal went off about forty-five minutes later. Later, we found out that Charlie had tried to sneak under our perimeter wire but the guys in the perimeter bunkers set off a claymore mine and killed six or seven of them. That was the end of their attack.

An Eagle's Eye View

22 February 69: After the attack on Camp Evans the previous night, we were really working hard to finish up our bunkers. We also added more layers of sandbags and PSP (perforated steel plank) to the top of our bunker.

Before we left Colorado, we had to have complete physical and dental checkups. After seeing the base dentist, he said some of my fillings needed to be replaced. I had the dental work done. I suffered all day long with a toothache, which was really hard to endure while shoveling sand.

Camp Evans, expecting to be hit again, was put on yellow alert. This meant that everyone carried around their weapons with them, no matter where they went. Because we were on yellow alert, some of our guys had to pull guard duty around our company area and the gully where our aircraft were to be parked.

23 February 69: On this day we continued filling sandbags, which lasted most of the day. The food in the mess hall was really terrible. We had a chance to go to the little PX (post exchange) on Camp Evans, and it was a big letdown. There were few items to choose from, especially when it came to something to eat, which was what I was really trying to find. I pulled guard duty that night for the first time. Pulling guard duty here was really scary because there are a lot of poisonous snakes in the brush. I watched over the area where our company's aircraft were to be parked in a gully on clear patches of dirt where they bulldozed the area. Brush still remained in-between and around the parking areas. There were no lights visible anywhere, and all you had to see by was starlight. Walking around there was not my idea of fun. It was raining and a section of our perimeter was getting hit. Charlie was trying to destroy our ammunition dumps. He did not succeed. They were firing illumination flares during the attack, and one of them fell short by our latrine. One of our motor pool personnel just happened to be in the latrine at the time. Thinking it was a mortar round, he was so messed up physically and mentally he had to go to the field hospital to get cleaned up and settled down. I was relieved, in both meanings of the word, when my three-hour shift on guard duty ended.

24 February 69: By this day, my jaw was really swollen, so the medic sent me to the field hospital on Camp Evans. I found out they will not fill teeth in a combat zone; instead, they just pull them. I would like to see the dentist from Colorado right about now because it was his handy work they removed. After I got back to our AO (area of operation), I helped find materials to build a shower. This was a "high priority" mission. None of us were able to take a real shower since our arrival. Living in a tent with a bunch of guys who did nothing but fill sandbags and sweat all day was a real bummer! Our temporary shower consisted of 55-gallon drums on the roof of the framed-in shower stalls. The water temperature was the same as the outside air temperature. We had hot showers when it was hot and cold showers when it was cloudy or rainy.

25 February 69: Today the 1st Sergeant informed us that if we were caught with a loaded weapon on Camp Evans, there would be a $100.00 fine. When I first heard this, I thought he was joking. He also said that we did not have to wear our steel pots (helmets) around the company area anymore, which was a relief. We received word that our aircraft would be arriving soon in Da Nang and we're scheduled

Tien Sha

to fly down there the next day. We spent the rest of the day filling sandbags again, and my jaw was still very tender from yesterday's ordeal.

26 February 69: We left for Da Nang at 1:30 p.m. Our aircraft were due to come in on the Navy ship. We flew in a Chinook and landed at Red Beach. Then we loaded on trucks and went on to Tien Sha. Tien Sha was really nice. Arrangements were made to put us up temporarily with a Sea Bees' outfit. They had a new two-story air-conditioned building and a swimming pool. This was great. The best part was the mess hall; the cook actually asked you how you wanted your eggs prepared with other choices besides, which is unheard of in the Army.

27 February 69: Our aircraft still had not arrived, so we were able to go swimming in the South China Sea. I could not believe how salty the water was. Later on that evening while in the mess hall, we heard that Charlie blew up a Navy LST boat and killed fourteen sailors.

28 February 69:   Early that morning, Charlie hit the base with mortar rounds and B-40 rockets. One of them hit a ship loaded with gunpowder in the harbor just a little ways from the

Artillery Flares

Sea Bees' camp, and the concussion from the explosion really rocked the building where we were staying. The bed I was in slid twenty feet across the floor to the other side of the room. Another one of Charlie's rounds hit the ammo dump, which caused multiple explosions, setting off rounds stored in the dump for over an hour after the initial hit. There was a lot of firing coming from the bunkers on the perimeter of the base. The explosions were really lighting up the sky. The artillery was shooting illumination flares so the guys in the bunkers could see what they were shooting at. This action is how I had pictured being in Vietnam would really be like. I was amazed how unaffected I felt after that morning. Throughout the rest of the day we just continued waiting for our aircraft to show up. Some of us went swimming in the pool and we took advantage of the mess hall. This was almost like being on R&R (rest and relaxation). I only wished I could have taken that mess hall back with me to Camp Evans! Those Navy cooks sure could cook! I had never been asked or given choices of what I wanted for breakfast, lunch, or dinner the whole time I was in the Army.

01 March 69: Since our aircraft still had not shown up, Gene and I spent the day swimming in the pool they had there. That night we went to go see *To Hell With Heroes*, a war picture in a war zone. The movie was good, but Roger Olsson, who we called the Swede, and Tony, two of our crew chiefs, went into town the day before with some sailors to have a few drinks. The few drinks led to a few more and when they came out of the bar, it was dark. At Tien Sha they locked all the gates up at night, so Swede and Tony knew they were in trouble. The sailors had driven a pickup truck with bench seats in the back for passengers. The three sailors sat up in front, and Swede and Tony had to get in the back. When they started driving down the road back to camp, snipers started shooting at them. Swede, Tony, nor the sailors had weapons with them. The two in the back both tried to hide underneath the narrow, wooden seats. That was not much cover for those two. The sailor drove on the street and sidewalks trying to hit the VC (vietcong) that were shooting at them. They were lucky enough to have made it to a Marine compound that was in the center of the city, which just so happened to be under attack as well. Fortunately the Marines opened the gate and let them in. They sat with their backs to a wall, making that night a very long one. The Marines fought the VC until dawn. During the night, the VC blew up a bridge on the road back to Tien Sha, so on Swede's and Tony's return, part of the trip was by boat. When they finally returned, they were confined to base because they were off base without permission after dark. They remained confined until we returned to Camp Evans. They really didn't need to do that because I think that trip to town really cured them both.

02 March 69: Our CO asked me to go with him to the PXs at China Beach and Red Beach. These turned out to be really nice, just like the ones we had state side. The main reason the "old man" (CO) invited me along was to provide security for him with my M-16 rifle. After what Swede and Tony went through, all of us were being a lot more careful on our trips outside of camp. There was still no word as to when our aircraft would arrive. I spent the rest of that afternoon swimming in the pool.

03 March 69: We were finally notified that the ship with our aircraft was out in the harbor but would have to wait its turn to unload down at the docks. The Navy estimated that it would take two more days before they had an open pier.

I decided to go see the city of Da Nang. It looks like a ghetto. The teenagers looked like they were ten years old. Some of them would give us the peace sign, others would give us the finger, and a few would throw rocks at us when our backs were turned. Friendly folks. Walking around, trying to watch your back, wasn't very enjoyable, and I only saw one modern building in the whole city. I went back to camp and swam in the swimming pool some more.

04 March 69: One of the things I have to mention is the smell here is horrible. This bothers me more than anything and I can never get use to it. The only time I could ever get away from it was when we were flying in the air. They used human excrement in South Vietnam to fertilize their fields. Sanitation didn't have a very high priority. Trying to stay alive was their main concern. I wish the people who think the air is polluted in the United States could experience the odors to which we were subjected.

Our CO informed us that the ship we were waiting for would dock the next day. This generated some excitement and gave us good reason to go to the club and celebrate.

05 March 69: This was the day we were waiting for; our aircraft finally arrived. They were all wrapped up in camouflage tarps. Removing all of the tarps from our aircraft was a lot of hard work. After I worked for some time, I finally uncovered the one I had been looking for, 658. I was glad to see it again. I now had something to work on instead of filling sandbags. We finished removing all of the tarps, but it took us almost all day to accomplish this task. From what we could tell, the helicopters all looked like they had made the trip without any damage. Working in the heat and humidity of South Vietnam seemed to make everything twice as hard. You could not drink enough water, and we had to always take salt pills twice a day to replace what we had lost in our systems. I could never get use to the heat and humidity. Despite the working conditions, we were all in a better mood that evening, and we were anxious to start working on them again the next morning.

06 March 69: The night before Charlie hit us again with a bunch of rockets. They had Sea Bees repairing the damaged PSP and also filling in the craters where the rockets hit the runways. After breakfast we loaded up in the trucks and headed down to the docks. Having been shipped across the

Author; at Tien Sha heading for 658 to mop off the salt residue after its boat ride to South Vietnam

Pacific Ocean, the first thing we had to do to our aircraft was completely wash them down with clean water. This cleansing removed the corrosive salt which could have damaged our aircraft. After cleaning 658 I had to install its gun mounts. For shipment they were strapped down to the inside of the aircraft. My personal toolbox was also with the aircraft, so I was able to go right to work. I unstrapped the mounts from the floor of 658 and found the hardware to attach them. After I finished installing the M-60 gun mounts, the tail rotor blades were next. I had to wait while the maintenance people finished up on the one they were working on because we only had one set of rolling scaffold. While I was setting up the tail rotor blades for installation, the heavy maintenance people started to install the main rotor blades on 658. I took my time

Gene Parks

with the tail rotor and really did a good job. The old man came by and told me that since I was so fast, I could be in charge of installing the rest of the tail rotors on our aircraft. That was fine by me. I was enjoying doing something constructive for a change. I finished one other aircraft that day, but my sergeant said I'd have some help the following day.

07 March 69: They assigned Gene Parks to work with me. He was from our maintenance section, but he was also a friend of mine. Gene and I met at Fort Carson when we both had KP (kitchen police) duty on the same day. We were peeling potatoes. All you actually had to do was cut out the black spots or sprouts and then put them in an automatic potato peeler. After we loaded it up, we started talking and when the Mess Sergeant came to check on them, they were the size of golf balls. He cursed for a while and then brought us each another 100-pound bag to start all over again. We thought this was funny but the Mess Sergeant didn't. What could they do, send us to Vietnam? We were already going there.

That morning Gene and I found the scaffold and went to work installing the tail rotors. By the end of the day we had four more aircraft with tail rotor assemblies on them. While we were working on our aircraft, we were staying in the air-conditioned quarters of the Sea Bees stationed there. When they came back from wherever they were that day, they kicked us out. We had to move our gear and live in tents the rest of the time we were down there.

That night Charlie mortared us again. His main targets were the aircraft out by the main runway. The base was so big he had plenty of targets at which to shoot. Some incoming rounds were mortars, but the big ones were B-40 rockets. When the rockets went off they really got your attention, because they were about ten times as loud as the mortars. It was hard to write in my journal because the concussions were shaking the tent, cot, and also the candle I was using for light.

08 March 69: Trying to sleep last night was really hard. My cot kept shaking every time a rocket would hit. Since there weren't any sandbags around our tent, I went outside and watched the fireworks. If anything hit close, I'd be hit anyway, so I decided I'd like to see it coming instead of lying there waiting for it. The gunships were up flying and the rockets and mini-gunfire going off at night were really something to see. The gunfire looked like a steady stream of red, even though there were four regular rounds between each of the tracer rounds. I wouldn't want to be on the receiving end of that. After breakfast, we headed down to the docks where Gene and I continued installing the tail rotors. While we were working, the Major (CO) came by and told me that I'd been promoted to Specialist 5th class. This was good news because it meant an increase of pay. Also, this was a chance to celebrate for a good reason, instead of the ones we'd make up.

09 March 69: Gene and I had breakfast and we caught a ride down to the dock with some MPs (military police). We installed five tail rotor assemblies today and that was the best day so far. I also received mail from home for the first time. The Major came by and told me I was doing a good job getting things done. We should be finished with all the aircraft by tomorrow. Our pilots and crew chiefs that stayed back at Camp Evans showed up today. I don't think they ever want to see another sandbag again.

10 March 69: Gene and I finished installing the last of the tail rotors. I was glad to get off that hot PSP. We'd been roasted, toasted and grilled the whole time working down there at the dock. Gene and I went to the China Beach PX, where I bought a nice Minolta camera and some food and booze to take back with me to Camp Evans. While we were there, they took 658 out on its test flight and everything checked out ok.

11 March 69: Dan and Ed showed up at 658 early that morning, and we had our first up close view of the countryside while flying back to Camp Evans. Since we didn't have our M-60's with us, we flew out over the ocean out of rifle range. We also hadn't been issued any Nomex (fireproof) flight suits, so we had to fly in our jungle fatigues. The only thing the Army did issue us in the states was our Nomex flight gloves.

Being back in the air again was really nice. I hadn't realized how much I missed flying until then. Everything on 658 was working great. Dan and Ed told me our radio call sign for our company was "Lancer." This made our landing pad back at Camp Evans "Lancer Pad." When we got closer to Camp

Temporary Parking Pads

Evans, the weather started to get worse. There was rain, fog and poor visibility. The visibility was down to a quarter mile. We landed at Lancer Pad and parked 658 in its assigned area. I tied it down and closed everything up to keep it dry. Since the weather was bad we stayed inside cleaning our weapons. I had guard duty that night so I wound up sloshing around in the mud again. One good thing was that while we were gone, the Sea Bees came and built our permanent hooches. Swede and I moved our gear into the hooch assigned to the 2nd flight platoon.

Swede was one of the first friends I made when arriving at Fort Carson. We were pretty close friends by now. When I first met him he told me he came over to the U.S. on a work visa from Sweden. He was working as a mechanic here for a while and was drafted into the Army. He wasn't even an American citizen and he'd already been through his military obligation in Sweden. When he came here, Uncle Sam got him again. I still can't figure that one out. While we were in Colorado and everyone was getting leave passes to go home before we

Don Bullock, Ed Ellison, Roger Olsson (Swede) & David Mussey warming up by the fire!

went to Vietnam, they didn't want Swede to go home because Sweden was a neutral country. The Army thought he wouldn't come back if he went home. They finally let him go, and he did come back. He said the funny part was when he arrived in Sweden and took a bus to go to his parents house, the people on the bus started talking bad about the U.S. and him in Swedish. Since he was dressed in his military uniform for travel, they mistook him for an American. After listening to all the negative comments, he told me that just before he got off the bus, he spoke in perfect Swedish and told all the people on the bus what he thought about them.

12 March 69: I woke up to pull guard duty again and it was still raining and cold. I continued to slosh around in the mud most of the day. That evening Swede and I discussed the advantages of keeping a journal. Even though we were single at the time, we both thought that it would be nice to let our kids know what we went through. After this I decided to keep on writing in my journal.

Dan, Ed, and some of the other pilots were sent down to Camp Eagle for in-country flight training. They were supposed to be gone for a couple of weeks. Gene pulled guard duty that night, and he told me that the radar they had in the bunkers picked up two tigers walking around the outer perimeter.

13 March 69: I worked on 658 in the rain as usual. I pulled the intake screens off and cleaned out all of the dirt. Our airfield was not sealed with tar yet, so everything became dusty and dirty real quick when it wasn't raining. We had a lot of rats lately and set a few traps in our hooch and bunker. We finally caught one in our bunker, and it was almost as big as a cat. We heard today that one of the crew chiefs in A Company was killed on a mission. They arrived earlier than we had, so they were already flying combat missions. I pulled guard duty again from seven to eleven, and then hit the sack.

14 March 69: I went to the armorer and checked out the M-60's assigned to 658. I spent the day dismantling, inspecting, and cleaning them. After that, I found some Plexiglas cleaner and cleaned all the windows and shin bubbles on the aircraft. Because of all the rain and mud, I had to clean every place I had to stand on to wash the windows. I felt like I was spinning my wheels. I decided it was time to drink beer.

15 March 69: Even though the weather was bad; keeping all of our aircraft grounded, the 1st Sergeant had us filling more sandbags again. He had the other crew chiefs pulling company details because his clerks complained that they were supposedly doing all the work and the flight crews weren't doing anything.

16 March 69: We continued filling sandbags and this was sure getting old. Finally, after the clouds lifted, they sent us on a flight to Camp Eagle. We took one of our officers down there for some reason. We had to wait a couple of hours for him to accomplish his errands, and while we were waiting the weather worsened. On our flight back to Camp Evans, I had to fly with my door open so I could help the pilots look for wires crossing over Highway 1. The bottom of the clouds were only about forty feet above the ground, so we had to fly above the highway to avoid hitting any trees. We had to fly slowly, and I became really soaked hanging outside. A few times we could barely see the road below us and we weren't that far above it. I was glad when we made it back to Camp Evans. That was the coldest I have ever been since being here. I didn't need to take a shower that night.

17 March 69: We tore down some buildings for lumber this morning and this afternoon. I built a wall locker for Swede and me. We installed a light bulb inside to keep our clothes dry. If they just hung out in the open, they would start growing mold on them in three days or so. Finally the sun came out and seeing it again sure was nice. I hoped we would start flying soon. Everyone was getting on each other's nerves. I went over to the maintenance hooch and drank beer with Gene and the maintenance guys. The only time I usually saw them was when I was in the hanger for some reason.

18 March 69: The engineers started working on our new airfield and parking revetments. They sprayed tar over the dirt and the airfield was a mess, but when the tar set up, it sure was going to be a lot better. There would not be as much dust flying around when we took off and landed. I hoped we'd start flying soon. We needed something to break the monotony of sitting around. No mail today. The mail we received from home was looked forward to by all of us. Reading the letters took our minds away from the war and the loneliness we all felt. I would read and re-read letters until new ones arrived. It was our only link to a civilized way of living and thinking. When they talked about the troubles they were having at home, that usually brought a smile to my face. If they only knew! Every time I went out flying and sat behind the M-60 machine gun, I felt like I had a sign on me that read, "aim here." That was something to worry about (if you were the worrying kind).

19 March 69: I stayed away from 658 today. The tar was still sticky and hadn't set up yet. I decided to go down to the PX at Camp Evans and see if they had anything good to eat. We already had a saying here, "The food in the mess hall would gag a maggot." When I came over to Vietnam I weighed 186 pounds and now I weigh 165. I wrote home to mom, asking her to send me vitamin pills and anything edible that wouldn't spoil in the mail.

20 March 69: Their monsoon here is really something. When it rains it sounds like rocks hitting our metal roof. I'll need pontoons on my helicopter if it doesn't stop raining soon. Our locker is working great, our clothes aren't growing mold on them any more. We are actually sleeping inside our sleeping bags at night. This won't last for long. There isn't a whole lot to do but to visit with each other since we're not able to fly missions yet. I got a letter from Shane today. Shane is a buddy of mine stationed in Quan Loi. We graduated high school together in Pinetop, Arizona. We were surprised to meet again in basic training at Fort Bliss, Texas. We both thought that "this is a small world," for there were only 28 seniors in our graduating class. We also wound up going through helicopter training together at Fort Eustis, Virginia. After we finished our training there, Shane received orders to go to Vietnam, and I was sent to Fort Hood, Texas. Shane is a Crew Chief on a cobra gunship and he liked it that way because all he had to do was fix it, not fly with it. He doesn't have too much time left over here, and he's happy about that. He said they'd get rocketed there daily and he won't miss that at all.

21 March 69: Today they brought over a conex container loaded with ammo. I got enough M-60 ammo to fill both boxes. I loaded them up and placed them inside 658 so they wouldn't get wet. There was also ammo for our .38 caliber pistols so Swede and I shot empty beer cans all afternoon. While we were down by the ammo conex I found an old bayonet. The handle was broken and it was all rusty. I took it down to the motor pool and used their grinder to clean it up. I decided to make a throwing knife out of it. In order to get out of the Army five months early, I decided to extend my tour until 15 April 1970, only increasing my stay in Vietnam by forty-five days. I felt it would be better than doing five months of stateside duty.

I wrote home that the food was terrible. I asked my mom to send me some Jiffy Pop Popcorn in the aluminum pan and some great big Hershey bars with almonds. I also asked for some *Field and Stream* magazines. No mail today.

22 March 69: The weather is still bad here. The clouds are really low. Since we didn't have any flights today, I went to the PX and bought some pieces of leather to make a handle for my throwing knife. I found a piece of plywood and I practiced throwing it at night in my hooch. I flew with it my whole tour of duty. Rumor had it that our door gunners would be showing up soon. When they arrived, we would be able to go on regular missions.

Our pilots came back from Camp Eagle. Dan said his first mission was what I refer to later on as a "no-name" mission. He said they had a team in trouble out by what we called the "Arrowhead." The team was in heavy contact when he and the others arrived, and his ship was designated the pickup ship. When they went in, they had to pick up the team with ropes. He said it was really an orientation flight.

23 March 69: We flew around Camp Evans today and parked 658 on the new field. It's a lot nicer now. We parked our aircraft between rows of fifty-five gallon drum barrels that were filled with sand to protect them from rocket and mortar rounds. It was a pretty close fit for them but Dan and Ed had no trouble at all parking 658 between the barrels. I hadn't seen either one of them for a while so we just sat in 658 and talked. Both these officers were well liked because they treated everyone the same. Ed was a few years older than Dan and I, and he had some good stories. He was an awesome pool player too. Swede and I saw him win a lot of money in the bars in Colorado. Dan was the quiet one but he managed to get in trouble just like the rest of us. I got him in trouble once but what are friends for? Sorry Dan! This story is told on 11 May 69.

Our New Lancer Pad

24 March 69: I decided since we weren't flying to take advantage of all that ammo in the conex. Swede and I took our M-16's down to our little firing range and did some target practice. Some of the pilots joined us, and it was a lot of fun. I zeroed in my M-16 and it was shooting great. I found twenty empty magazines and loaded all of them up. I found some bandoliers and put the loaded magazines in them. I carried these with me when I flew. If we were ever shot down, I wanted to be prepared. After that we went back to the hooch and cleaned our M-16's. Finally some of the door gunners started coming in; although I hadn't been assigned one yet. I did a little cleaning on 658.

25 March 69: The 1st Sergeant had us cleaning up the company area. Last night one of our sergeants got drunk and while stumbling around in the dark, he fell down in the gully. He broke his arm and was banged up pretty good. He was sent back home to the States. Some of the guys started planning that night's events. Get as drunk as they can and see if they can be as lucky as he was. Since the clouds and rain left, it started to become hot here. We still couldn't fly any missions until all of our door gunners showed up. The days were going by slow because we just continued waiting and doing petty details they gave us to keep busy.

The Gully by our Company Area

An Eagle's Eye View

26 March 69: I checked the flight schedule the night before and we were to fly 658. When Dan and Ed came out to the flight line, I asked them where we were flying. They said Battalion wanted the pilots to familiarize themselves with the area around Camp Evans. I went and checked out the M-60's while Dan and Ed were doing their pre-flight inspection on 658. When I returned, Ed helped me put on the M-60's while Dan finished up the pre-flight inspection. We installed both M-60's even though we didn't have any door gunners yet. We hoped that if Charlie could see both guns, he would think we had a full crew.

Villagers waiting to collect their dinner

We took off from Camp Evans and first flew west towards the foothills. We wanted to get a close look at the mountains rising up behind them. When we were near the mountains we could see the start of the heavy jungle. It looked really pretty and green but also uninviting at the same time. We then headed north to see what it looked like. There were more hills and bigger mountains visible the further north we flew. We then headed east towards the ocean, and the closer we came to it, the countryside became flatter. There were a lot more villages near the ocean. We hadn't seen any flying west or north.

When we started getting close to the water, I told Dan and Ed this would be a good time to get rid of the rusty ammo in the cans. If you didn't use up your ammo in a week or so, the links holding the shells together would start rusting. This was the start of our fishing trips. You could see sharks swimming around all over the place, and it was perfect target practice. I was having fun. Dan and Ed decided they wanted to shoot so I traded places with Ed, and he shot while I got to fly. Then Dan traded with Ed and he finished shooting all the rusty ammo. During this time, the villagers started gathering on the beach. When they saw the sharks floating on the surface, they started dragging their boats down to the surf line. After we finished up firing all of our old ammo and started back for Camp Evans, they all waved at us as we flew over their village. I saw them launch their boats to go out and get their dinner. That was a fun day, and I didn't mind cleaning the M-60's. I at least had a chance to shoot them this time. We had to clean our M-60's after every flight whether we shot them or not because of the moisture.

Perfume River flowing through the City of Hue

27 March 69: I found out we were scheduled to fly our first night flight. It was to be another training flight for the pilots. We took off from Lancer Pad after dark and flew in a formation of five, south towards the city of Hue. We circled Hue and while flying back over the city, we started taking enemy fire from a .51-caliber machine gun. Those green .51 caliber tracers looked like basketballs coming up at you. Since Hue was a friendly city, we couldn't return fire. The only thing we could do was break up our formation and make it harder for them to zero in on us. One aircraft in our flight took a hit from one of the tracers. It didn't hit anything major, so we all made it back to Lancer Pad at Camp Evans. Those .51 caliber bullets make a nasty size hole. It's almost big enough to put your fist through. Swede and I worked on our helicopters until three in the morning doing our maintenance check and performing our pre-flight inspection. We were ready to fly again.

28 March 69: After last night's lesson (being shot at), I spent most of the day taping up 658's navigational lights so they could only be seen by another aircraft that was flying with us at the same altitude or above us. All the other crew chiefs did the same on their aircraft and this was the start of our combat training. Learn as you go and adapt.

29 March 69: I cleaned 658, and we also got paid. Swede bought a Swedish machine gun from a grunt (infantry soldier), and he is like a kid with a new toy. I also received a copy of my Spec 5 orders. I planned on going to church again the following day. I went last Sunday and it was nice.

Sambo River outside Camp Evans

30 March 69: They put us on battalion standby. We flew down to Camp Eagle twice. We flew some officers down there the first flight and made a parts run the second. It started raining again that afternoon, and it was nice and cool outside.

Swede & his Swedish Machine Gun

Sure felt good. Swede and I drank beer and shot the breeze.

31 March 69: My pilots still needed more cross-country flight time. So we flew down to Phu Bai and went to their main PX. We flew back to Camp Evans over the ocean, and between the ocean and Camp Evans, I received another flight lesson. I was getting better.

01 April 69: I pulled guard duty. Helicopter 658 is due for its twenty-five hour inspection. I took oil samples from the transmission, 42-degree gearbox, and 90-degree gearbox. These were then sent stateside to be analyzed for metal-wear of the internal components. If anything unusual showed up, you were notified and took the necessary steps to repair the problem. I also checked the rest of the components listed on the twenty-five hour inspection sheet.

We were finally assigned door gunners. The one I got is from Nebraska and his name is Terry Lee Gerke. He came out on the flight line while I was working on 658. We introduced ourselves, and I asked him where he came from. He said he

Terry Gerke by 658

was from a line company and was also a pathfinder. I asked him why he volunteered to be a door gunner, and he said he'd heard that door gunners only had a life expectancy of thirty days. He decided to take his chances flying. The Infantry Company he was with was using him as a night LP (listening post) man. I asked him what that was, and he said they sent him out at night alone with a radio away from their company

Terry Gerke & Dan Shea on 658

position to listen for enemy movement. If he heard any, he was to call in artillery strikes on the enemy position. *(I didn't realize this until later but sometimes our artillery didn't hit where it was directed at: they called them short rounds. I'm sure the guys on the ground called it, and them, something else.)* This sounded to be a pretty good reason for wanting to be a door gunner. I took Gerke over to where the company armorer was set up and showed him the M-60's assigned to 658. He said he'd like to check them over, and I told him to meet me back at 658 when he was finished so I could show him what he needed to know and explain what his duties were when we were flying. Later on that day, Gerke came back to 658. I then showed him how the radio worked for his flight helmet. I explained the body armor we wore and what it would stop. I told him he would be sitting on the right side of the aircraft and the reason for that was so I could see the aircraft gauges, which were only visible from the left rear side. Then I went over the flight procedures. I explained that before the pilot started the aircraft, it was our job to make sure everything, especially the main and tail rotors, were clear of obstructions. I told him the pilots would ask us if it was clear. I then said I would check the tail rotor, which was on my side and the main rotor blade on my side, and if everything was clear, I would say "clear left." If everything on his side was clear, he would say "clear right." Then I told him when the helicopter reached operating speed and we were ready to take off, the pilot would say, "we're coming up." Our response would be "clear left and clear right" if it was ok to take off. I then told him we didn't lock and load the M-60's until we cleared the outer perimeter fence. There was nothing else I could add at this time for we hadn't been on any combat missions yet. Having Gerke on our crew was really a comfort to the rest of us. We had someone who we looked up to for his experience in combat, someone who would teach us the ropes and guide us through. We all felt we had a better chance of making it with him on the crew.

02 April 69: They put us on maintenance standby. If our heavy maintenance crew needed any parts from our main support group at Camp Eagle, we were on call to pick up those parts. We made one trip down to Camp Eagle on a parts run. Gerke was doing fine, and the machine guns were really clean.

03 April 69: We were put on maintenance standby again, but we were diverted to help search for a downed aircraft near Camp Eagle. It was one of the Air Calvary helicopters that was shot down. This unit would send one helicopter out, and he would fly at treetop level and try to draw enemy fire. If he did, he would call in his position and the assault section of the unit would drop troops right on top of Charlie's position. They knew the general area he was working in but he went down so fast he didn't have time to radio in his exact position. We flew for over four hours searching for the helicopter, but we never saw anything. Some of the other aircraft involved in the search took some heavy enemy fire, and some of the ships took hits and had to return to Camp Eagle for repairs.

04 April 69: We flew up around the A Shau Valley; it was a really rugged looking place. It was green with giant bomb craters scattered along the valley floor that were filled with water. There are some large-sized mountains on both sides of that valley, which runs north and south. The Laotian border runs along the top of the mountains west of the valley. This valley was also one of the main supply routes from North Vietnam to South Vietnam. During the monsoon season, Charlie owned it completely. The Americans would pull out of the valley before the monsoon started because of the impossibility of resupplying field units either by air or land during that season. The clouds would come right down on top of the trees, and any road would turn into a mud bog with no bottom. We flew supplies out to fire bases: Veghel, Whip, Bastogne, Burmingham and Sally. Sure hate to go down out there.

05 April 69: The weather was really socked in so no flights. Swede and I were getting real tired of sleeping on our cots. They weren't very comfortable at all. We had made some friends who are with the artillery unit on the hill above our AO (area of operation), and they had some extra mattresses they gave us. So we scrounged up a bunch of lumber and built some bunk beds that would hold our new mattresses. We could now roll over in bed without falling out of it. We even had enough lumber left to make a table to cook our food on. Swede liked the mess hall about as much as I did. Every time we wrote home, we asked them to send us food. When our care packages did arrive, we'd eat in style until it was gone. Some of the foodstuff they sent from Sweden I couldn't hack, but they made some potent liquor.

06 April 69: It was Easter Sunday, and we had to fly our first combat assault mission. We left Camp Evans and flew to a staging area in the A Shau Valley where we landed. Our 2nd

Our First Combat Assault Mission

flight platoon leader was then briefed on the mission. He came back and had to brief our pilots. That was when Ed and Dan told us there would be a slight delay because they had to use the Navy to prep the LZ (landing zone) with their guns. We didn't have any artillery close enough to reach the area. Waiting is really hard on the nerves when you're scared. We finally got the signal to crank up, the troops loaded onboard, and we took off. When we started getting close to the landing zone, I saw a waterfall coming off the mountain, which looked really pretty and green. Then it was gone. There was nothing left but dirt and tree stumps. The naval shells were still hitting the LZ when we were getting ready to start our final approach. I then heard our flight leader say, "I hope the Navy shuts that off before we get there." This landing zone turned out to be a really tough one to get into. When our turn came we had to guide the pilots in because of the tree branches. We had to come in and down, then back and down, then forward and down to get close enough to the ground to drop off the infantry. We chopped some branches going in and out, and we were talking constantly to the pilots telling them to either come left or right depending on how thick the branches were on either side. Ed flew us in the first time, while Dan was helping Gerke and me guide him in and out. After we made it out and were heading back toward the staging area to pick up another load, Ed told Dan, "it's your turn." We made the next lift and this time, Ed helped us guide Dan through the branches to get into the LZ.

    The concentration it took these guys to get us in and out of there was really something. There wasn't a whole lot of room either way and a mistake by either one of them would have caused 658 to crash. I can't say enough about the skills

A Shau Valley

Sombo River, this area was called Lazy W

of these two pilots; to be flying and hearing trees being chopped while still holding it steady, still amazes me today when I think of it. There were also a lot of other Lancer aircraft involved in the CA (combat assault). Each one of them was going through the same thing we were, which tells of the quality and skill of the rest of the pilots and crews in our company. None of our aircraft were damaged. This was the start of the bonding men have for each other when your life is in their hands and their life is in your hands. To say I was scared is an understatement, but we made it through our first combat assault mission. Thank You Lord!

07 April 69: Our 2nd flight platoon leader, who was a Captain, flew my aircraft. He was taking turns flying all the helicopters in the 2nd flight platoon. This means we were flying lead ship. It was another combat assault mission. Only this time, we were hauling ARVNS (the army of the Republic of South Vietnam soldiers).

Cobra Gun Ship Flying Escort

We flew them up further north in the A Shau Valley than the previous day. We picked up our first load at the staging area and took off. As we approached the LZ, the cobra gunships started firing rockets and mini-guns to prep it and to keep Charlie's head down if he was close. This was a new experience, watching the rockets fly by and explode right in front of us.

We came to a hover, and the ARVNS were really slow getting off. I guess they didn't know we were a prime target, and we felt like sitting ducks. My platoon leader started screaming, "Are we up; are we up," and I said, "They're just taking their time getting off." Finally they were out, and I told him we were up. At least it wasn't a hot LZ. On our way back to get another load, I told my door gunner that the next time in we'd get up and help them out. On our next trip in, when we got close to the top of the elephant grass, Gerke and I got out of our seats, and we started unloading. Before we came to a hover, I told the platoon leader we were up; he just nosed the aircraft over and we were gone. This became another SOP (standard operation procedure) when hauling ARVNS out in the field. On our way out of the LZ, I looked back and saw Swede and his gunner doing the same thing. When I saw Swede later that night, I asked him if he had trouble the first time in too. He said yes, but when he saw me and my door gunner unloading them the second time, he knew that was the answer to that problem. The Americans we hauled couldn't get off fast enough because they knew they were safer on the ground. I couldn't speak Vietnamese so if they didn't get off quick, they were helped. It was for their safety as much as it was for ours. Some ARVN outfits were trained really well and no help was needed. I guess it just depended on their officers.

An Eagle's Eye View

After our combat assault mission we flew to one of the firebases in the A Shau Valley. Our next mission was to rig 658 with spray equipment.

Two of the new fire bases had a lot of vegetation around them so we were loaded up with a defoliant (agent orange) for the spray rigs; and we spent the rest of the afternoon flying circles around these bases, spraying. This was done to increase the bases, clear field of fire and also so they could detect enemy movement at night before the enemy got too close. It was a long day of flying. We flew back to Camp Evans and I did the maintenance work on 658.

08 April 69: We went on what I'm going to call a "no name mission." It was something altogether new to us. Three aircraft from our 2nd flight platoon, including 658, were volunteered for this mission. We flew from Camp Evans to "their" camp. After we landed, their people came out and rigged each one of our aircraft with four repelling ropes. We were told we were taking a four-man team on an insertion. One aircraft would carry the team, and the other two would fly what we call "chase." If anyone got shot down, the chase ships would pick them up on the ground or use the ropes if needed. This mission also consisted of four to six Marine UH-1B model gunships or, on other missions, a combination of Marine and Army gunships.

We had an Air Force control officer in a fixed-wing aircraft running the operation. There was also F-4's (airforce phantom jets) on station if we needed them. When we saw all the firepower they were using on this mission, we started to get a bad feeling because on our previous combat missions, we only had two gunships with us. When Dan and Ed came out of the briefing, they didn't look too happy. Dan said we didn't have to go on this mission; it was a voluntary one. I asked if he and Ed were going, and he said, "Yes." I really trusted these two pilots, so I said "I'm in," and Gerke said it was ok with him. We were assigned to be one of the chase ships. When their team came out to load up on the insertion aircraft, they were all dressed in enemy uniforms and were carrying enemy weapons. After seeing this, the "pucker factor" for this mission went up three notches. Dan and Ed told us not to shoot at anything during the flight unless they gave us the word. They wanted to insert this team as quietly as possible. It was a long flight to the LZ, but we made it there and back without shooting or being shot at, which was fine with me. We landed back at their camp, where they removed their gear they had installed, and we were released to fly back to Camp Evans. I did my usual maintenance routine.

09 April 69: We pulled several combat assault missions. All of them were located in the A Shau Valley. We went in shooting on some of these and had a lot of trouble with the M-60's jamming. They wouldn't feed right with that flex belt. Also, the bag they used to catch the empty shell casings would catch the wind and just whip the M-60 all over. When we got back to Camp Evans, Gerke and I got rid of the bags; I figured it was better to have empty shell casings hitting the tail rotor than live bullets hitting us. Another "learn and adapt" lesson. Worked on 658.

Gene came by and told me that he and A.W. Smith decided to try and get on flight status. Yesterday, they had outhouse duties and that was their deciding factor. I'll explain what these duties entailed. There are several outhouses scattered around our company area. Fifty-five gallon drums were cut in half and placed under each seat. There was a trap door on the outside of the building where they could be pulled out. After you pulled them out far enough from the building, you poured diesel fuel in the cut drum and ignited it. While it was burning, you had to stir it so all the contents would burn up into ashes. After doing this all day, you smelled just like the contents in the can. Your friends avoided you until you hit the showers, and that is as deep into this subject as I'm going to get!

10 April 69: We were assigned another "no name" mission again. Gerke had company duties, so one of the sergeants was flying as my door gunner. I wasn't too happy about this but it gets better. We left Camp Evans and flew up to "their" camp. Ed was my pilot, but I don't remember who my co-pilot was. The briefing on this mission was quite detailed.

It was also the first I was ever allowed to attend. They informed us that this mission was going to be an extraction. They had a team in trouble. They had a map of the area with markings on it all over the place where the PZ (pickup zone) was. It was explained that some marks were SAM (surface to air missile) sites and the others were anti-aircraft battery sites.

It seemed to me that by looking at their map you could avoid some of the dangerous zones but not the others. They then told us it was a four-man team. They said they were dressed in enemy uniforms and were carrying enemy weapons. If we saw more than four at the PZ, it was a trap; we were told to start shooting and get the hell out of there quick. They also said 658 would be the primary pickup ship with the other two Slicks (UH-1H's) flying chase. As if I wasn't scared enough, they had to tell me all of this before we went on the mission. I decided then I didn't like briefings. There were three ships from our 2nd flight platoon involved in the operation. They had their people rig all of our ships with four ropes each; when this was completed, we took off from their camp and headed for the PZ. We were getting close to the PZ and flying around 5,000 feet when I started to see black puffs of smoke. Suddenly, 658 started shaking like a giant had a hold of us. Ed asked what that was and I said, "I think it's antiaircraft fire." He took evasive action and changed altitude in a hurry.

When we got close to the team, we could hear the fire fight going on down below in the jungle. Some of our gunships went on ahead of us and started laying down fire around the team. The FAC (forward air controller) pilot directed us right over the team. I could barely see them through the branches and the undergrowth. I counted only three at first, but then I saw the fourth one lying on the ground. I dropped the ropes and grabbed my M-16. I had to lie on the floor so I could see under 658; this way, I could direct the pilot to keep us right above the team. Two of the guys were trying to get the ropes untangled from the trees while the other one was shooting at Charlie; the fourth guy was just lying there. I had two magazines taped together for my M-16, and I fired all the rounds I had in both. This seemed like it was taking forever. The most welcomed site during this ordeal was the Marine B model gunships that were flying in a tight circle around us. The door gunners were hanging completely outside their helicopters, held only by a harness firing their infantry style M-60's from their shoulders. The cobra gunships were flying a little further out firing their mini-guns and rockets into the jungle around us. Even with all this firepower being directed at the enemy, he was still in heavy contact with the team we

An Eagle's Eye View

were picking up. Finally, the two guys had the guy who was laying on the ground hooked up and were working on getting themselves hooked up, while the fourth guy covered them. Then the fourth guy got hooked up. By that time, the only thing I had left to shoot was my .38 pistol, so I emptied that in the direction from where they were taking the most fire. They finally gave me a signal when they were ready, and I told

No Name Mission: Team on Ropes

the pilot to take them straight up. We had to clear some 200-foot tall trees before we could go forward. As we were pulling them straight up, one of the team members had his AK-47 (Russian automatic weapon) on full automatic and was shooting and spinning around like a top. When we cleared the trees, I told the pilot he could get the hell out of there. When we were a mile away from the PZ, I could hear the bombs the jets were dropping where we had picked up the team. A little later, we could hear the B-52 bombers unload. It was a continuous rumbling sound.

On our way back, Ed asked my gunner what was wrong with his M-60. He said nothing was wrong with it. Ed then asked him why he didn't shoot when we were in the PZ, and he said he didn't see anything to shoot at. I'd been so busy during the extraction that I didn't even notice he wasn't firing. This made me mad because the guys on the ground sure could have used some help, and it also left his side wide open for us to take fire. I checked the guys on the ropes and I told Ed we had one guy hit pretty hard, just hanging limp. I told him we'd better set them down as quick as we could and get them inside. They located an abandoned firebase and had the gunships rocket and mini-gun a spot for us to land. This would set off any surprises Charlie would have left. We hovered at 250 feet and set them on the ground. I cut the ropes, and then we landed as close to them as we could. I jumped out to help them aboard. All four of them were wounded, and one was seriously wounded. While all this was going on, my gunner just sat there; now I was really getting pissed off. We took off from the abandoned fire base, and I got down the first aid kit we carried. One of the team members and I started to work on the one team member that was hit hardest. We had almost gotten the bleeding stopped when my door gunner said, "Gee Terry, I didn't know you were a medic." I started to get up off the floor but Ed turned and must have seen my face because he said, "Terry don't do it," that stopped me and I calmed down and finished patching the guy up. One of the guys on the team asked for water. They said they'd been chased for a day and half and had run out of water the day before. I had four canteens under my seat, so I handed them out. They had

Mess Hall with Hanger in background at Camp Evans

medics waiting at their camp when we landed, and they took the team from there. When we got back to Camp Evans, I found my Platoon Sergeant and told him, in very colorful words, that never again would that sergeant set foot on my aircraft.

11 April 69: Finally I got to rest. I washed some clothes. We had to boil them in a .50-caliber ammo can and it worked pretty well. I worked part of the day on 658. We had some action while Gene was pulling night bunker guard duty. He said he kept hearing something rattle the cans we had hanging on our perimeter wire. He said it took them awhile to get permission to free-fire for two minutes, but finally they

Author; washing clothes

gave the "ok." When they went out to check the perimeter wire in the morning, when it was light enough to see, it turned out to be a Bengal tiger. I'm sure glad it didn't get into camp; it was bad enough with the Mess Sergeant trying to kill us.

12 April 69: When the other crew chiefs and door gunners found out someone was going to the PX in Da Nang, they came with their money and a list. The only problem was that enlisted men could only purchase two-fifths of booze a month.

An Eagle's Eye View

On their flight down, the crew chief said he asked the pilots if they would purchase the extra booze he had on his list (there was no limit on alcohol purchases for officers). They told him they both had big lists themselves. When they landed in Da Nang, one of the officers told the crew chief to take off his rank insignia and to put on an extra set of officer's bars he brought with him on his hat. The crew chief said this worked great. He was able to buy everything on his list. He said the only real problem he had was remembering to return the salutes he was getting from the enlisted men in Da Nang.

At Camp Evans, you didn't salute the officers because it made them a target for snipers. There were some exceptions to this, and we had a few in our company. We didn't mind saluting them at all. We figured if he needed that military courtesy and respect that bad for his ego, he could handle anything Charlie shot at him.

Food items on the list were the most important. The food they were cooking in our mess hall was all canned goods left over from the Korean conflict. It tasted like it too. The fresh eggs they would fry up for us were so old the yokes were white. I found out once when I pulled KP that they were packed in egg pack (looks like liquid vaseline), and they were as old as I was. I was twenty-one years old at the time.

I was living on C-rations and mayday soup that you could buy at the PX at Camp Evans. This kept me going until I discovered LRRP (long range recon patrol) rations. They were freeze-dried food in packets, only two years old, and all you had to do was add hot water. When the ship came back from Da Nang, we all collected our goodies. None of us went near the mess hall. We were set!

13 April 69: I worked on 658. Working on it during the day is harder than at night. The metal gets so hot you get burnt every time you touch something. You can't leave your tools in the sun or when you pick them up you get branded. I decided to clean the internal turbine stator vanes. I had to find Ed so he could run it up for me. To do this, I had to take the intake screens off the front of the engine, climb on top of the helicopter with it running, and pour crushed walnut shells into the engine intake. After the walnut shells went through, I poured ten gallons of water through it. This really cleaned them up and made it easier to check for damage or cracks in the vanes. This also helped the performance of the engine.

14 April 69: Our new flight platoon leader decided he liked flying 658 the best, so it looked like I had a new Aircraft Commander. I didn't like it very much because now I'd be the first one in on the next combat assault mission we get. We flew down to Hue and flew some Colonels around who were marshalling a parade from the air. I didn't know what the parade was for, but the military personnel guarding the parade route far outnumbered the parade participants. It was probably part of our "win their hearts and minds" campaign. It reminded me of the protest parades I'd seen on TV taken in the south with the National Guard on the streets.

15 April 69: We flew down to Phu Bai to pick up parts our maintenance people needed. They were not flying 658 very much because it was getting close to the 100-hour periodic inspection, which would take it out of service for two to three days.

16 April 69: We flew out to Little Vega, a fire base for the artillery guys on the hill behind us at Camp Evans. On our third trip out to Vega we shut down and ate. The pilots went with other officers to eat so Gerke and I went and ate with the grunts. I always carried a case of C-rations in the cargo compartment in case we got stuck some place and needed something to eat. The grunts were using C-4 (plastic explosives) to heat their meals. They just broke off a piece from the C-4 block and lit it with a match. It burned white hot and heated a can of C-rations in about a minute.

While we were eating, some of the guys told us about a snake they came across on patrol. They said they thought it was a log they were crawling over until it moved. They said they shot it with their M-16's but finally had to kill it with a M-79 grenade launcher. They said the head on it was so big it could have easily swallowed one of them or a good size deer. After hearing this, I was glad I was flying and not walking around in the jungle.

They asked us if we wanted some C-4 to take with us to heat our meals, but I didn't want to carry it in the cargo compartment. If a bullet hit it, we'd be vaporized. I asked one of them about the M-79 grenade launcher and how effective it was. He told me you didn't even need the launcher. He said if you took the round and threw it like a football, after so many revolutions, it armed itself and would go off when it hit. He then picked one up and threw it. He was right. I thought he would get in trouble for throwing it but nobody even seemed to care. I decided I would remember that and try it sometime when we were out flying. We finished our supply missions and when we returned to Camp Evans, I worked on 658. It had been six days since I'd received any mail.

17 April 69: We had division standby so we flew down to Camp Eagle. There wasn't much going on so we mainly sat around BS-ing all day. They released us in the afternoon so we flew back to Camp Evans.

18 April 69: We flew civilians around, spooks (CIA), for MacV. We flew mainly around the city of Hue. It seemed funny to be in Hue. When we first arrived in country, all the towns around our camp were off limits to us. Before we arrived, some soldiers from our camp got into a fight with some soldiers from another outfit. The fight escalated into a shooting battle. After that they declared everything off limits, except other military installations, to the guys at Camp Evans. This was the first full day I actually had any contact with the civilian population near Camp Evans. Most of the people seemed shy but very respectful. I did see two young men who, by their looks and actions, gave me a bad feeling. I kept an eye on them until we flew out of that area. I had a feeling they were converted VC the spooks were using for information.

19 April 69: To keep the hours down on my aircraft, flight operations put us on maintenance stand down. Camp Evans finally set up a laundry service so I didn't have to boil my clothes any more. I took them all down to be washed. I stopped by the PX and they had piles of beer in the back. They were all loose cans separated by the brand names. The PX had so many cans of Miller beer, that it was only fifty cents for a sandbag full. I was loaded down on my way back. Swede and I had bought a small refrigerator from a guy leaving so now we could have cold beer, if we could keep the generator running. They said they'd have my clothes ready by five that evening. I went back to get my clean clothes, and it was worth the $2.50 they charged me. That cold beer put me to sleep early.

20 April 69: Flying with the platoon leader does have its benefits. He gets to pick the missions he wants to fly on. We were assigned battalion courier flights. We picked up a good-looking Captain. She was the first white woman I'd seen since

An Eagle's Eye View

I arrived in February. Her perfume really got me thinking about home. We also picked up a Japanese girl who was wearing a miniskirt. That was cruel and unusual punishment for all of us on the crew but not one of us complained one bit. We were flying them out to a hospital ship that was cruising out in the South China Sea. This was really new to all of us; we'd never landed on a ship before. When we started to get close to the ship, my pilot contacted them for landing instructions. They explained the landing procedure to him and said the seas were rough so it would be tricky. The deck was pitching eight feet with the seas. When we were above the designated landing area, we had to synchronize our movement with the ship's. The trick was to land on the deck the moment the ship started on its way down. You had to land fast and solid so the sailors could tie you down before it started up again. This was scary.

After we landed, the sailors tied us down to the deck. Our pilots were then invited to go below deck, but Gerke and I were ordered to stay on 658 by our platoon leader. Dan and Ed would have taken us with them. Gerke and I didn't like RLOs (real live officers); they thought they were better than we were just because they had officer's bars. Almost all of the Warrant Officers treated their crews as equals. Military regulations did forbid officers from associating with enlisted men, but that is one thing I could never really figure out. The way I saw it, we were all in the same boat so we should all row the same. Two hours later, our pilots came back and were talking to another officer about how good the food they just had was. After I heard that, I didn't like my platoon leader one bit. We untied the main rotor blades and started 658. We took off without any problems and headed back for Camp

Evans. When we got back, Gerke and I went to the mess hall but passed on what they had for dinner. C-rations looked more edible.

21 April 69: After yesterday's flight, 658 was due for its next 100-hour periodic inspection. We towed it into the hanger, and the maintenance people started taking off all the inspection panels. Their tech inspectors would go over everything first and then have their people make the necessary repairs found during the inspection.

The last periodic inspection performed was before we left Fort Carson when it had ninety-eight hours. The total flight time on 658 at this point was 200 flight hours. Before they closed the inspection panels when they were finished, I visually checked all the repairs performed.

Gene Parks and A.W. "Root Beer" Smith had started crewing a few weeks ago, but hadn't been assigned any combat assault missions up to this point. They came over from our maintenance section; we had a shortage of crew chiefs because of people being transferred out of our unit or a few who took themselves off of flight status. Since we had all come over as a unit, the Army was shipping people out to different units so when our tour of duty was over (twelve months), the whole unit wouldn't rotate back to the states at the same time. Gene and A.W. found out they were flying on their first combat assault mission. A.W. came over and borrowed some of my flight gear since I wouldn't be flying for a few days. He also told me our platoon leader was flying his ship, and he had a lot of questions about what to expect. I filled him in the best I could.

22 April 69: I was working on 658 in the hanger when I heard we had ships in trouble. I went to flight operations and there was

An Eagle's Eye View

already a crowd listening to the radio communications of our flight involved in the mission. It wasn't good news; we had two aircraft down in the LZ. It was located in the foothills near the DMZ (demilitarized zone). I saw Dan there, and he said it was pretty bad, having been listening to the operation for a while. The pilots were shouting on the radios so we knew things were really turning to shit fast. We called it a "Cluster F." Since Gene was on one of the helicopters shot down that day and Swede was crewing the C&C (command and control) ship flown by our company commander, the rest of this day's story will be told according to them.

Swede said they were circling the LZ in the C&C ship when they saw the lead ship, which Captain John Scarlett and Bob Stroud were piloting and A.W. was crewing. He said they either landed on a mine or had a mine detonated underneath the aircraft on A.W.'s side, killing him instantly and wounding the rest of the crew. After the explosion Swede saw the door gunner, who was on fire at that time, trying to help the pilots, who were also on fire, out of the front of the aircraft. A Marine helicopter finally went in and picked up the surviving crew. After the crew was picked up, the Air Force was called in to make napalm runs on the LZ. On their initial run, the Air Force pilots saw someone waving a green and yellow scarf (the kind the ARVN troops wore). They broke off their run because they thought there were still friendlies alive in the LZ.

Upon hearing this, Gene's Aircraft Commander Jerry Cartier was at Cam Lo, the staging area for the operation, volunteered to go pick up the survivors. They took off from Cam Lo and flew over to the LZ, where they circled while Jerry contacted the C&C ship. After circling for what seemed like forever, they finally went into the LZ. On their final approach, the whole mountainside lit up with machine gunfire. Gene returned fire with his M-60 and didn't remember even hearing it fire until it jammed. That was the loudest click he ever heard. He then heard Jerry say they were hit, and the helicopter started to spin. After they dropped to the ground, they started taking heavy fire from the area directly in front of the ship. Jerry was struggling in his seat to get out of his harness, but when Gene worked his way over to him to pull the emergency release handles, Jerry had already managed to free himself. Gene grabbed his M-16 and took cover with the rest of the crew. At this point, they knew that it must have been over for Root Beer.

Jerry managed to obtain a radio from one of the ARVNs still on the ground and contacted the C&C ship. The commanding officer told them to prepare for the inevitability of spending the night on the LZ. Upon hearing this, Gene and his door gunner started back to their downed aircraft to get their M-60's. At this time, Ron Snyder, flying another one of Lancer's aircraft, landed to pick up the remaining survivors at the LZ. Everyone started running towards the aircraft and when they boarded, anyone who was able to started putting out covering fire as they took off. After they pulled Gene out, the Air Force went in and dropped napalm all around the LZ.

When the Air Force finished their bombing runs, another one of our Lancer aircraft, crewed by Mike Dorris and piloted by Ed Sakenes, landed in the LZ. Mike and his gunner got out of their aircraft and ran to A.W.'s to see if they could recover his body. The Air Force didn't get everyone because during this time their aircraft was taking multiple hits from small arms fire. When Mike reached the aircraft and tried to remove A.W., he couldn't pick him up because his body was jellified from the concussion. Mike grabbed A.W.'s dog tags and they came right through his neck like nothing was there. While this was happening, Mike's door gunner was wounded, and Mike had to carry him back to their aircraft. They loaded up and took off.

I'd like to say at this point in time, we had not been issued our Nomex flight suits, which would have kept Captain Scarlett's crew from being burnt. The suits miraculously showed up less than a week later, and we all thought this was to protect our battalion commander's butt.

23 April 69: Everyone was in a daze. I still couldn't believe A.W. was dead. That would have been me in that LZ if 658 hadn't been down for maintenance. A.W. was crewing Swede's ship that day; they'd made Swede a temporary line Sergeant while one of our regular Sergeants was on leave. We both felt like we had dodged the bullet that day. When one of your friends was killed, you started to think about your own life and what was in store for you down the road. I did some serious soul searching and what I decided was due to my religious beliefs: I knew my life was in God's hands and if He wanted to take me, He would; if I made it through this war, I figured He had other plans for my life. So with this attitude and belief, I kept flying. This, however, did not keep me from being scared more than a few times in my twelve months of flying.

24 April 69: I worked on 658 most of the day. The periodic inspection was finished, and the test flight was performed and passed. I was still pretty depressed about the loss of A.W. Another one of our crew chiefs in the 2nd flight platoon was talking about quitting and going back to maintenance. When we were crewing back at Fort Carson, they used to tell us if you screwed up, it was zip back to maintenance. Over here, it was the other way around.

That night, Charlie hit our perimeter, and D Company sent up some Cobra gunships to engage him. Everyone who worked back at Camp Evans headed for the bunkers while a few of us crew chiefs and door gunners got out our lawn chairs and drank beer while watching the gunships hose down Charlie with mini-gunfire and rockets. At night, this was a real fireworks show. It was nice to know someone else was on the other end of it for a change. I think I'm finally getting use to the war. If I only had some Jiffy Pop!

25 April 69: I didn't have any flights scheduled so I caught a ride down to Camp Eagle to look for a friend of mine I met in helicopter maintenance school at Fort Eustis, Virginia. I didn't have any luck finding him because he was out flying on a mission so I caught a ride back to Camp Evans. I received some mail.

26 April 69: We lost another crew chief. If this shit kept up, we'd all be dead before too long. Staff Sergeant Dorsey's helicopter was on a combat assault mission in the mountains by the A Shau Valley. They were just coming into the LZ when Charlie hit his side of the aircraft with an RPG (rocket propelled grenade), killing him instantly. The rest of the crew was hurt, but they made it out of the helicopter before it burned up.

The LZ was too hot to get the rest of the crew out, so they wound up spending the night on the ground. I felt for them. Just a few days before, I remember Sergeant Dorsey showing me pictures of his new baby daughter. It's a shame that she'll never know her father. This war was starting to really suck.

27 April 69: Since our platoon leader was wounded and sent back to the states, Ed was back flying 658. I was glad.

I really didn't like the idea of flying lead ship all the time. Our platoon leader wasn't a bad pilot, but I trusted Ed and Dan a lot more. We flew log (resupply) missions today. We resupplied some of the fire bases and hauled out their mail. They finally pulled out the rest of the crew that got shot down the day before. They said the only thing left of their aircraft was part of the transmission. The rest of it had burned up completely.

28 April 69: Another "no name" mission. Note: On a prior "no name" mission we had a chance to talk to Marine door gunners, and they showed us their M-60's and how they were set up. They had special feeder mechanisms, which eliminated the flex belt we had to use on ours. They had a standard-size can of C-rations clipped on the M-60 below the feeder mechanism. This let the belted ammo smoothly feed into the feeder. All you had to do was use your left hand and guide it a little bit. They also explained to us the reason why their rate of fire was a lot faster than ours. Their armorers used special buffers and springs, which they made for their ejection systems on the M-60's. We tried at that time to talk them out of some, but Swede only managed to get a feeder mechanism from one of them, which our company armorer was trying to duplicate for us.

When I found out 658 was scheduled to go on another "no name" mission and I'd be seeing the Marines again, I grabbed a fifth of Jack Daniels whiskey and wrapped it up in an old T-shirt. I then stored it in my cargo compartment on 658. Their camp was so far north the only thing they ever got was beer; I hoped this would work. When we landed at their camp and we were waiting for the briefing to start, I saw a Marine walking by. I called him over and explained what I was looking for. I told him I needed two feeder mechanisms and two buffers with the springs they used in their M-60 machine guns. He asked me what I had to trade for them. I told him I had a fifth of Jack Daniels "whiskey" and before I finished saying whiskey he was gone. He came back less than five minutes later with everything I wanted. He carried that fifth away like it was made of gold. I'd made one Marine very happy. Now we could set up our M-60's so they'd work. Gerke couldn't wait to get back to Camp Evans to install the new toys. After this, it didn't take the rest of our company's flight crews very long to also obtain upgrades through the barter system.

    We then went to our briefing which at the start of it, they told us the weather was too bad for any missions so they were canceled. Those were the best words I'd heard all day. The tension left all of us after that announcement. We flew back to Camp Evans. Gerke took the M-60's and the new parts and headed for the armorer's shack to clean them up and install the new parts. He then went looking for some larger ammo cans for 658. We finally were able to get rid of the little cans they gave us because we didn't need to use the flex belt anymore. He came back with some empty .50-caliber ammo cans, which more than doubled the amount of ammo we could carry. We used some heavy tie down straps to anchor them to the gun mounts. No more running out of bullets in a hot LZ.

    29 April 69: Swede flew as my door gunner, and Gerke was glad to get the day off. We flew a bunch of Civilian Engineers around; they were looking at all the bridges on Highway 1 that crossed the rivers in our AO. It was a pretty easy day. When we got back to Camp Evans, we found out it was payday. We first did the maintenance needed on 658, and then we collected our pay and went to the NCO (non

An Eagle's Eye View

commissioned officers) club. Swede, Gene and I got pretty drunk, and I also knew I didn't have to fly tomorrow.

30 April 69: Woke up with a hangover. Swede and I spent the day cleaning up our living quarters. Everything in our hooch got dirty real quick. It paid to keep it clean because those rats we had are mean looking suckers. There was no telling what you'd get if one of them happened to bite you. If we'd hear a yell in the middle of the night we knew one of the other guys just had a rat run across him. It paid to keep your living area clean. We also used our mosquito nets to cover us up at night. Before the Sea Bees came and built our new screened-in hooches, if you had a light on you could see

Swede at Fire Base Blaze

hundreds of bugs crawling all over it. And each one of them was different.

01 May 69: We were assigned log missions. We carried out mail and food rations to the guys on some of the fire bases. There were quite a few new fire bases being built or enlarged out near the A Shau Valley. It was a spooky place out there, and I always had an eerie feeling when flying around out there, like something bad was just waiting to happen.

02 May 69: We continued flying more log missions. We flew six hours, hauling supplies out to the bases near the A Shau Valley; they were getting ready for something out there. When I returned to Camp Evans, I found out they had one of our birds taking guys to Coco Beach to go swimming. That sounded pretty good to me. I grabbed my M-16 and a bandolier of ammo, and jumped on board the shuttle aircraft. Cold beer and a cold dunk in the ocean sounded good after

The Beach

flying all morning. The beach had a lifeguard and was pretty secure, but you still took your M-16 out there with you and kept it close at hand. The only thing missing on the beach was the opposite sex. After my dip in the ocean, I flew back to Camp Evans on the shuttle aircraft. I stowed my M-16 back on 658 and did my post-flight maintenance routine.

03 May 69: We flew several sorties (flights) out to Fire Base Blaze. This place was really getting big. They even set up a new refueling pad for our aircraft. They were really stockpiling the artillery shells. There was a lot of CH-47 traffic constantly coming and going with sling load after sling load of everything they needed for their support of the guys in the field. When we completed our sorties, we flew back to Camp Evans and I did my maintenance work on 658.

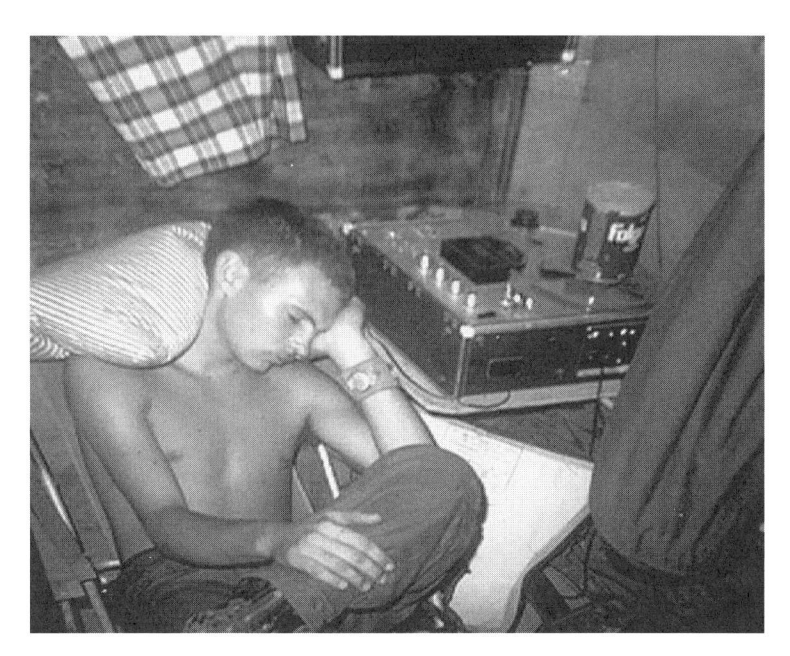

Author; listening to the new sound system

04 May 69: We were all grounded because of the weather. Swede and I went to the PX and bought a tape recorder; it sure sounded good. We were both real pleased with it since we could tape the good songs off of the radio and send tapes home that we recorded. My brothers could also send us music from the states. Everyone was getting tired of listening to the albums I brought over. Gene came over and we all drank and enjoyed the new sound system.

05 May 69: The weather was still bad so there were no flights. I decided to clean 658. I gathered up some buckets of water and soap, and Gerke and I cleaned the exterior. It looked a lot better. The exhaust from the turbine engine really turns the tail boom black. Hopefully we'd stay a little bit cleaner when we climbed all over it to do our maintenance work. I met Swede later on and we went to the NCO club.

06 May 69: A Special Forces unit (green berets) needed two of our aircraft for a few days. They sent us on 658 and another aircraft from the 2nd flight platoon TDY (temporary duty) to their base. We moved some elements of their unit to several different LZs close to the Laotian border. Some of these places were really tough to get into. One of the LZs turned out to be a hot one, so we aborted the insertion and took them to a secondary LZ. We were flying without any gunship cover so it made for a real tense day. We all felt drained when we made it back to their camp just before dark. I completed what maintenance checks I could before it became too dark to see. They told us they had sandwiches for us for dinner. These guys had real ham with lettuce, tomatoes and good bread. And here we were out in the middle of nowhere in a Montagnard village. We stuffed ourselves. After eating, I went out to make sure 658 was secured. I met one of the Special Forces members who was on guard duty. I didn't feel very safe because there were no visible defenses. There just didn't seem to be anything to stop Charlie from coming in and blowing our ships up (and us with them). I asked the guard if we should sleep in our aircraft and rotate on guard duty. He then told me they wanted both crews to stay in the tent they had assigned us, and he said they didn't want us coming out until it was light or one of them came for us. He continued to say, they had Montagnards around the camp in the jungle, and they could smell Charlie and there was no way he could get by them without the Special Forces team knowing about it. I'd seen some of them when we first landed. They were carrying crossbows and blowguns. They weren't more than a little over four feet tall, but they had that hard look you get when you've seen a lot of combat. I believed him and none of us left the tent that night.

07 May 69: The food we had for breakfast was far better than anything we had at Camp Evans. After we ate and were getting ready to take off, I saw all the villagers in the stream. It was like something out of National Geographic Magazine. They were all naked, splashing around taking a bath in the water. They were so small they looked like kids with grownup faces.

We flew some of their Special Forces people to Fire Base Hickory. It was really back in the boondocks near Khe San. This place was situated on top of a cliff, and at the base of this cliff were several wrecked helicopters. Going in and out of Hickory was really a trip with wind shears and downdrafts. I now know why there were so many wrecked helicopters at the bottom of the cliff. Ed and Dan didn't like this place one bit. After this mission it was back to Camp Evans. I was sure glad to get out of that area.

When we got back, I found out that Gene had won the Air

Medal with the V Device for valor due to his actions the day he was shot down.

08 May 69: We flew some log missions in the morning, and I worked on 658 the rest of the day. We started to get a lot of new pilots that just arrived in country, so the crew of 658 was being broken up. The CO had made both Dan and Ed Aircraft Commanders. I told them both I sure didn't like the idea of flying with someone else. I had a lot of faith and trust in them, and I didn't want some green pilot flying me around. They told me they'd try to fly my aircraft as much as they could. Ed was my main Aircraft Commander after this point, but Dan also tried to fly 658 when Ed wasn't scheduled.

I ran out of food to eat so I went to the mess hall to see what they had for dinner. It was chicken. They were processed whole and put into a gallon can. I think the cook just warmed it up because when I bit into the chicken it was bloody and raw.

09 May 69: I had a mild case of ptomaine poisoning and I was sicker than a dog. That was the last time I ever ate meat that came out of a can in the mess hall. I stayed in bed the whole day.

Gene came by and told me that when his door gunner was loading up to go on their mission he accidentally put four rounds through the roof of the helicopter and into the main rotor blades. He got shot down before he even left. Gene thinks he did it on purpose.

10 May 69: This day marked the beginning of Operation Apache Snow. We went into the A Shau Valley in force. There

An Eagle's Eye View

Initial lift for Operation Apache Snow

Heading for LZ

Operation Apache Snow LZ

F-4 Air Strike near Hamburger Hill

An Eagle's Eye View

were close to seventy UH-1H helicopters at the staging area and over twenty helicopter gunships. I'd never seen so many troops and helicopters in one place at the same time. There were several LZs we were going to hit, and we were told it was a free-fire zone the first time in. There were no friendlies on the ground anywhere we were going. Fear of the unknown or what might happen started working on you. We all had that feeling you get in your gut again. All the LZs we were going to were close to the Laotian boarder. There was no doubt in our minds that some of these LZs would be hot. Laos was Charlie's sanctuary.

If we hit some really hot LZs, we'd have F-4s on call. The crew on 658 was Ed, the new co-pilot, Gerke and myself. All morning long flights of UH-1H helicopters were arriving and parking in their assigned places at the staging area. Several flights of gunships also landed at this time. When they gave us the signal to load and crank up, the noise from close to 100 helicopters running was awesome. Charlie must have thought the whole U.S. Army was coming after him. The first LZ we hit was quiet, and we made two trips into it. The next LZ was the same. The third LZ we hit we took fire coming in and going out. I guess Charlie couldn't pass up all these targets he had and the initial shock of troops being dropped off all over the place probably wore off. We didn't take any hits, but we could hear the sound of AK-47s, which are very distinctive with a cracking like sound. Charlie fired some RPG's at some of our aircraft. I saw one go streaking underneath ours when we had just left the LZ. Those really get your attention, especially when you're the one sitting on top of the fuel cell for the helicopter.

11 May 69: We had another big lift into the A Shau Valley. Dan was my Aircraft Commander, and he had a new pilot with him. Ed got the day off; I wish I did. I don't like flying out in the valley. We continued to insert troops. We were taking some reinforcements to one LZ and Command said it was secured. People had been on the ground there since yesterday. As we were coming in on our final approach to land, Charlie started shooting hot and heavy. Dan broke off our approach, and we got out of harm's way. He talked to the guys on the ground and told them he was contacting some of our gunships we had on call. He also gave the guys on the ground the radio frequency the gunships were using so they could direct their fire where it was needed when they showed up.

We only circled around for five minutes or so waiting, and pretty soon we had two Cobra gunships as escorts. The guys on the ground were telling them where to concentrate their fire. Gerke and I didn't shoot on the way in because we had gunships on both sides of us. We dropped off their replacements and made it out without taking any hits. Our next LZ was a new one, and it wasn't a very good one either. There were tall tree stumps all over the LZ site, and we had to guide Dan in and out of that one. We had to go to Fire Base Blaze to refuel several times that day. We all welcomed the chance to get out and move around a little. We also had a chance to eat, even if it was out of a can. We spent the rest of the afternoon inserting troops at different LZs all around the valley. Some of these were hot, and some cold, but not knowing what was coming was starting to wear on all of us.

At the end of the day, we all felt like we'd been through the grinding mill. When we returned to Camp Evans, Dan invited me over to his hooch for some beers. This sounded great. While I was in his hooch, one of the RLOs saw us. He didn't say anything to us at the time, but he went and told the "old man" that Dan was associating with an enlisted man.

Dan got his ass reamed out by the old man the next day. I saw Dan later that day, and he told me what had happened. I said, "No problem, from now on just come down to our hooch and

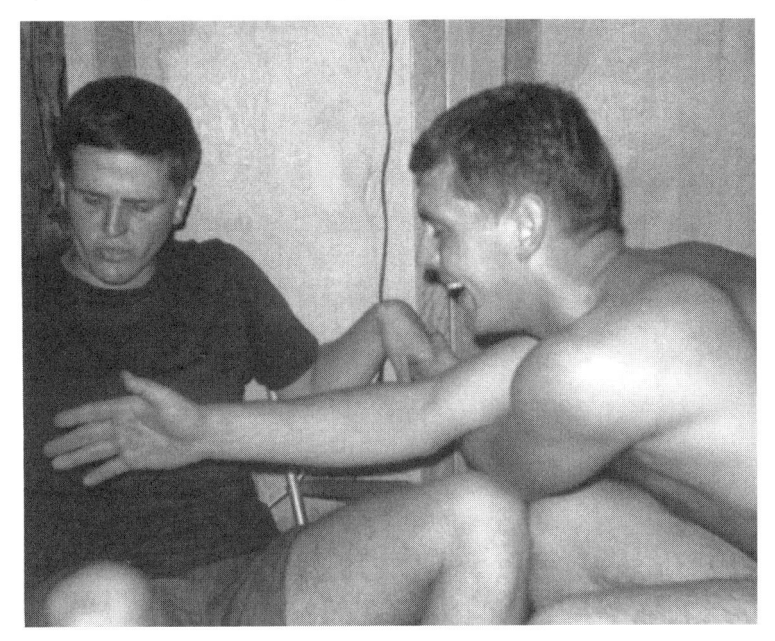

Dan Shea & Ed Sakenes

drink." None of the RLOs would be caught dead down there so he'd be safe. From then on, all the pilots came down to our hooch to drink. We had some great parties.

The only way to stay cool here was to wear your skivvies all the time. We spent most of the day dressed like this unless we were scheduled to fly or felt brave enough to go to the mess hall.

12 May 69: No flights were scheduled so I worked on 658 most of the day. It was a mess from the previous day's flight. I never sweated so much in my whole life. It felt like we were in hell working out on the flight line. Later on that evening,

Charlie fired a bunch of B-40 rockets at our camp, and he killed our outhouse. That'll save the shit burners some work tomorrow.

13 May 69: We had another "no name" mission. I thought to myself, "Here we go again," and I got that knot in my stomach. We left Camp Evans early in the morning and flew to their base camp. At the briefing that morning, they told us the mission was an extraction because they had another team in trouble. The only good part about this was that we were assigned to fly chase instead of being the pickup aircraft. Their briefing maps looked like the last I'd seen. There were markings all over the place showing enemy SAM and anti-aircraft sites. During the briefing their personnel installed their gear on the primary and secondary aircraft, which consisted of four 250-foot ropes they would be using to pick up the team. After the briefing, we were off to the PZ site. We made it to the PZ without taking any enemy fire of any kind. The secondary aircraft circled the PZ about a mile away while the primary pickup ship was extracting the team on the ropes. Everything went smoothly and we regrouped and headed back to their camp.

On the way back, we saw a SAM launch. It was like Cape Canaveral, only this one was coming out of the jungle. The FAC (forward air controller) told the F-4's about the missile launch; they just hit their afterburners and they were gone. Our flight dropped down to treetop level and started doing contour flying at 120 knots, which was the maximum speed for the UH-1H. We made it back to their camp without any more surprises. I said Camp Evans looked like a hellhole when I first saw it, but now it started to look like a fine place to be.

The following pictures were taken on our way back from some of the "no name mission" that we flew on.

An Eagle's Eye View

Cobra on "no name mission"

Refueling for "no name mission"

Abandon Marine Base Khe Sanh

South Vietnam & Laotian Border

14 May 69: We flew down to Phu Bai on a maintenance run because we needed more parts for our helicopters back at Camp Evans. On the flight down and back I took some pictures of the bridges and water buffalos because I promised my family back home I'd send them some pictures so they could see what the countryside looked like. I also had a chance to hit the PX at Phu Bai and restock my food supply. Forget the mess hall. When I returned from Phu Bai, I just had to clean the screens on 658.

15 May 69: We flew out to Fire Bases Eagle's Nest and Nuts. We flew several sorties to each hauling grunts and groceries. We put in a long day in the air. Gerke didn't have too much time left in country and he only had about six weeks of his tour remaining. I sure was going to miss flying with him. He was really good at his job and never complained about anything. I sure wish he'd stay, but I don't blame him one bit for wanting to get out of here and getting back to the world (USA), the land of flush toilets and hot and cold running water. It's amazing the small things you really miss.

16 May 69: We were scheduled for a combat assault mission. We were to insert troops around Hill 937 near the A Shau Valley (hamburger hill). Since this was going to be one of the biggest battles the 101st Airborne would ever be involved with in South Vietnam, I'll give you some insight as to what events lead up to this mission. One of the elements we inserted the 10th or 11th of this month came across a communications cable (five inches in diameter) going into Laos. They went in the opposite direction and found out it was coming from Hill 937, Dong Ap Bia on the map. What they didn't know at the time was how strong the enemy position really was. The NVA (North Vietnamese Army) had built it during the time they were fighting the French government. Their bunkers had 250-foot tall trees growing on top of them, and they were well concealed.

We picked up troops in the staging area in the A Shau Valley and headed for our first LZ. Since Swede's ship had crashed (the one root beer was crewing) and was waiting for a replacement, he was flying with me as my door gunner. Gerke didn't mind because he was getting short. Short means very little time left on your tour of duty. We flew over ten hours that day, inserting troops around Hill 937. We didn't hit any hot LZs, and that was fine with me. We went back to Camp Evans and worked on 658. It was easy when there were two crew chiefs doing the work.

17 May 69: We were scheduled for another combat assault mission. We flew out to Fire Base Blaze and picked up reinforcements for the units fighting on 937. They had an LZ open, and it was called LZ2.

It was on the side of Hill 937, and it was too steep to land. There were a lot of tree stumps sticking up, and Ed had to hover about five feet off the ground so the guys on board had to get on the skids and jump off. They had a lot of KIAs (killed in action) in bodybags ready for transport so Gerke and I had to stand on the skids and pull them into 658. After a few trips of hauling live ones in and KIAs out, we started hauling in food, ammo and water for the guys on 937. All morning long F-4's were bombing the top of 937. When the Air Force wasn't bombing it, the Army was hitting it with artillery barrages. The word we were hearing about the fighting was that Charlie had let a company advance between their bunkers, and when they had them in a crossfire, they opened

An Eagle's Eye View

Author; took this picture of LZ2

up on them. They said out of 184 men there were only 50 left who weren't killed or wounded. Now I know why I saw so many KIAs at LZ2. I was glad to get back to Camp Evans.

18 May 69: Dan was flying 658. We were going back to support the guys on 937 again. We picked up a load at Fire Base Blaze and headed for LZ2. Charlie was shooting at us all the way in until we dropped into a hole in the jungle canopy where LZ2 was. Since we already had troops on the ground in the LZ, we couldn't fire our M-60's going in or coming out for fear of hitting friendly forces. Gerke and I unloaded 658, and

Fire Base Blaze

Fire Base Airborne

An Eagle's Eye View

Fire Base Airborne

then we got set up to load more KIAs aboard. After we loaded more KIAs aboard, Dan brought us up, and as soon as we climbed above the trees, Charlie started shooting at us again. We headed back to the fire base and when we landed and were unloading the KIAs, a photographer came up to me and asked if he could go with us on our next trip. It didn't take the press long to get here. I told him it was all right by me, so I told Dan we had a passenger. He said he was from *Life* magazine and wanted to get some good pictures close up of the fighting. I didn't tell him the LZ was hot. When we got close to 937 and started our final approach, Charlie started shooting. I guess that photographer never heard live rounds zipping by him before. He went up behind the pilot seat and was trying to hide. Charlie was close that day because we were even getting fired at in the LZ. Gerke and I got out on the skids again and started loading KIAs. The grunts also threw up some captured

Troops at Fire Base Currahee

155's fire support mission; for troops on Hamburger Hill from Fire Base Currahee

An Eagle's Eye View

Dan Shea

weapons they wanted us to haul out. By this time, the photographer was trying to climb underneath Dan's seat. We got loaded and took off back to the fire base; on the way back, the photographer didn't say a word. He looked as white as a sheet. When we landed, he jumped off and we never saw him again. All of those fancy cameras he had and he didn't take one picture. He didn't even thank us for the ride! Before returning to Camp Evans, we made one more trip into LZ2 with the usual: ammo, C-rations and water.

I'm going to explain something now about the last two days that really needs to be said. Everytime the weight shifts in a helicopter, the pilot has to compensate for it. When Gerke and I both got on the same side of the aircraft and were on the skids pulling up the KIAs, the helicopter never even moved. If it had, the movement would have dumped Gerke and me on the stumps down below. Dan and Ed were that good.

19 May 69: Instead of pulling another combat assault mission, we were put on maintenance standby. They sent us down to Phu Bai on a parts run. While I was down in Phu Bai, I found out they finally recovered the ship A.W. was crewing, which was Swede's old aircraft, 659. I went over and took a look at it, and it was really messed up bad. When we returned to Camp Evans, there wasn't much to do on 658. It was an easy day for a change.

20 May 69: Another combat assault mission. We flew out to Fire Base Blaze. It looked like another big lift was going to take place. We were going to be inserting more troops around Hill 937. This time, we would be dropping them off higher on the mountain. We made a few sorties from Fire Base Blaze to different LZs on 937. Everything was quiet at these LZs. We were then sent to Fire Base Airborne to move troops from it to another LZ on 937. This one was a hot LZ. We took fire going in and heavy fire on the way out. At least we could shoot back this time since there were no friendlies in that area.

On our second flight in, one of the door gunners on one of our helicopters finally took out the enemy .51-caliber gun that was shooting at us. Hill 937 was really changing. Since this push started, they've been bombing it day and night. Most of the green vegetation was gone, leaving only dirt and shattered tree trunks sticking up. The ground was littered with the remains of the shattered trees. It was a long day of flying. I had a lot of work to do on 658 when we got back to Camp Evans. I didn't get much sleep.

21 May 69: We had another big lift on 937. We picked the guys up at the staging area and headed for Hamburger Hill. We were to land right near the top. When we started to get close, I started to see the concrete bunkers that Charlie had

An Eagle's Eye View

Leaving Hamburger after dropping troops on top

built. It was funny seeing them with tree stumps and several feet of dirt on top of them. There were still pockets of NVA around the LZ, but I think we took them by surprise. I could see their foxholes, and there was one underneath us where we were going to hover that had an NVA soldier in it. I pointed him out to the guys on board so they could take care of him when they got off. I couldn't shoot because he was directly underneath us. The guys got off, and we were gone before the NVA soldier had a chance to react. I think part of the reason he didn't shoot at us was the downwash from our main rotor blades created a miniature dust storm so he probably had his eyes closed to protect them from the flying dirt and debris. That was as close as I'd ever been to the enemy up to that point and time in my tour of duty. That was too close. We flew twelve hours that day. It was another late night working on 658. Swede left for Saigon to pick up his new aircraft.

22 May 69: Early in the morning, we flew a combat assault mission from Fire Base Blaze to an area near Fire Base Airborne. Throughout the rest of the day we resupplied the rest of the guys at Fire Base Airborne. It was another real long day of flying. We made it back to Camp Evans around eight or nine that evening. I went and found something to eat, and then I worked on 658 until early in the morning. I felt like a walking zombie from a lack of sleep.

23 May 69: We flew support for the guys on Hamburger Hill. All morning we were bringing in food, ammo, water and reinforcements to different LZs around the hill. I was having trouble staying awake. On one of the flights to one of the LZs from the fire base, I turned on the radio, and I remember listening to Glenn Campbell singing "Gentle On My Mind" as I propped my feet up on my M-60 and got comfortable. The next thing I knew my pilot was screaming, "Chief, are you hit? Are you hit?" I told him I wasn't hit; I was sleeping. He said, "they're shooting at us," and I said, "I'm so tired right now I don't care." He asked me why, and I told him I had only gotten eight hours sleep in the last three days. I could tell he was pretty upset with me until I explained the reason I'd fallen asleep. I told him it was easy for pilots; when we get back to Camp Evans, you grab your gear and you get to go to bed. He asked me how late we'd been working on 658 the last three days, so I told him. He said he didn't realize I was working that long after our flights. After this happened, the pilots would actually stay and help us do what they could so we each could get the same amount of sleep.

We then flew back to Camp Evans where the pilots picked up another helicopter and crew to finish the day so Gerke and I could get some rest. We still had to do our work on 658, but at least we went to bed long before midnight for a change instead of early in the morning.

24 May 69: Our guys on Hamburger Hill were still doing some heavy fighting with the NVA. We were assigned to the 2/506 as a medivac ship. It was really mentally hard hauling out the wounded. You could see the pain in some of their faces, while others were in shock with no expressions at all. It really makes you hurt inside seeing them like that. It affected all of us on the crew that day. Gerke and I tried to make them as comfortable as we could. We lit cigarettes for the guys that wanted to smoke and passed out water to those who were thirsty. On some of the flights we had to hold up the IV's the medics had on some of the wounded. We didn't waste any time on these flights to the hospital. Ed had it pegged at 120 knots going and coming back all day long. They were putting all the weapons of the wounded men on our aircraft with them. The hospital, however, didn't have a place for them so I stored them in my cargo compartment. I kept four of the M-16's for 658 and gave the rest of them to some of the other pilots. I also kept an M-79 grenade launcher, which I thought might come in handy one day.

25 May 69: We were assigned log missions to resupply some of the fire bases. While we were unloading at one of the fire bases, I saw an officer go up and talk to Dan, who was in the aircraft commander's seat. I couldn't hear the conversation

The top of Hamburger Hill

Top westside of Hamburger Hill

An Eagle's Eye View

because I was unplugged. Dan pointed back towards me, and the officer came over and asked me if we could pick up a sling load of bodies I hadn't even noticed was there. There were approximately nine or ten NVA bodies on a cargo net. The officer said they were enemy sappers who had attacked and killed some of our own guys the night before. I checked the fuel gauge to see how much fuel we had on board. Since we were only half full, I told him there wouldn't be any problem lifting them. I then asked him where he wanted us to take the

Wrecked Low Observation Helicopter Fire Base Airborne

bodies. He then pointed out a location in the A Shau Valley they believed to be an enemy base camp from where the sappers staged their attack. He told me he wanted us to drop the load right on top of this location. We hovered over the cargo net, which they hooked up to our cargo hook, and we took off for the drop point. I don't think any of us thought twice about what we were doing because we felt this would save American lives. Charlie might think twice about hitting our fire bases with sappers.

We then flew to Fire Base Airborne. There were some wrecked aircraft lying around the fire base, and it was a constant reminder of what could happen to you. This was the same area where Sergeant Dorsey was killed.

Later that evening, Swede made it back from Saigon with his new aircraft. I worked on 658 and then drank some beer with Swede.

26 May 69: We supported the 2/506 again. The A Shau Valley continued to change. They were building a road right into the valley to supply Fire Base Currahee. We flew eight

CH-47 dropping supplies off at Fire Base Currahee

hours resupplying the 2/506. After our log missions three of our aircraft, including 658, landed outside of Fire Base Currahee.

An Eagle's Eye View

CH-47 dropping supplies off at Fire Base Currahee

Cobra leaving refueling station at Fire Base Currahee

Our pilots were going to be briefed on a combat assault mission scheduled for the next morning. We walked up by the fire base, just as a platoon was coming in from the field. They had a guy on a stretcher, and he had a bullet hole right between his eyes with just one drop of blood underneath it I'd seen enough, so I went back to 658 while the pilots were being briefed. While they were in the briefing, Charlie started to rocket and mortar the fire base. I saw one guy go flying through the air; I then decided it was time to untie 658 and get it running. I was in the process of starting it up when my pilots came running up. Ed jumped in the other pilot's seat and took over the starting procedures while the other pilot jumped in back behind my machine gun. Mortar rounds were hitting all over the place, but we made it out of there in one hell of a hurry. We flew back to Camp Evans, which really started to look like a 4-star resort to me.

27 May 69: We were put on combat assault standby because the weather was too bad for any flights. I worked on 658 cleaning things up. After the last few days, I didn't mind the bad weather at all if it kept me on the ground back at Camp Evans.

28 May 69: We were scheduled for combat assault missions again. We found out we were pulling the guys off of Hamburger Hill. On our first flight in, I noticed it was more wartorn than that last time I was there. The guys on the ground were sure happy to see us. When we lifted off, you could see the relief in their faces knowing they were going back to a secure area. (If there was such a thing?) You could see the shift in their emotions as they started to reflect on what they'd been through. They were a somber bunch when we landed back at their camp. I don't recall how many trips we made that day but we flew 15.2 hours. The guys had sayings written on the camouflage covers of their steel helmets. One of these said, "I can live for weeks without mail, days without food, hours without water, minutes without air but not a second without ammo." Another one read, "when I go to Heaven I can already say I've spent my time in Hell." I think this one about summed it up for what these guys had been through.

29 May 69: Another combat assault mission. We made fifteen or sixteen trips, hauling fifty more grunts to the base of Hamburger Hill to bring a company back up to strength. Charlie was still around, and we took some fire going in and coming out. We also brought in the supplies they needed. That was another long day of flying.

30 May 69: We had battalion duties. We carried the pay officer, (a 2nd Lieutenant) around to the different fire bases. He wasn't scared when landing at fire bases this side of the mountains; but when flying out to Fire Base Currahee in the A Shau Valley, he started to look kind of peaked. We flew to all the fire bases in our AO. It was another long day of flying and I worked on 658 when we got back.

31 May 69: Helicopter 658 was on ASD (assigned stand-down day). We all got to rest. I was just getting ready to take my clothes to the laundry when my platoon sergeant came into the hooch and told me they needed 658 for a log mission. I asked him why. He said the aircraft scheduled had maintenance problems. He then told me he knew how much I'd flown in the last three days and that it was my ASD day. He asked me if I wouldn't mind if he put a whole new crew on 658 so that I could take my laundry in and get some rest. Since it was only a log mission, I said that they could take it. I never saw 658 again. When they came in, the crew said they were on final approach to Fire Base Eagle's Nest when a poncho liner blew up and wrapped around the tail rotor causing them to lose control and crash. When I first heard this I felt like I'd lost a trusted friend.

This ends the history of 658 as told in my journal.

Closure:

Helicopter 658 was taken to Phu Bai to our division maintenance repair section. A few days later we were notified that the repairs needed could not be performed in South Vietnam. It was going to be sent stateside back to the manufacturer. They assigned Ed to a new aircraft due to the shortage we had of qualified Aircraft Commanders. Reggie Kenner was the Crew Chief on the one Ed was assigned. Reggie told me that the only reason he's alive today is because of Ed's flight skills. On a mission while coming out of a hot LZ, the helicopter was shot up and started doing all kinds of crazy things in the air. He still doesn't know today how Ed managed to get them back into the LZ and on the ground without crashing.

Shortly after this happened, Ed's sister arrived in South Vietnam. She was a nurse in the military and since they had a policy that no two people from the same immediate family could be in a war zone at the same time, she told Ed to go home because her job was much safer.

When I returned from a flight one day Ed was already packed and gone. I never had a chance to say goodbye to him.

I'm sad to say that while doing research on this book I found out that Ed passed away a few years ago. *He is gone but not forgotten.*

Gerke spent the remainder of his tour bartending in the Officers Club. I miss flying with him he was the best door gunner I ever flew with in Vietnam.

Before Dan completed his twelve-month tour and was rotated back to the states, I did fly with him on different missions during the rest of my tour of duty.

Shortly thereafter, I went on R&R, came back to Camp Evans, and flew another nine months. Those are other stories to be told at a later date!

An Eagle's Eye View

After 658 had been repaired, it was put back into service stateside in the U.S. Army. The Firelands Military Museum purchased it from the Ohio National Guard, and they restored it to a flyable status.

The following pictures are of Fire Base Eagle's Nest and most of the crew members on 658 the day it crashed.

Fire Base Eagle's Nest

Fire Base Eagle's Nest

Dave Haglund – Door Gunner

Ron Snider – Pilot

An Eagle's Eye View

Left Mark Lennick–Crew Chief that day of the crash
Right Terry Willman not on 658 that day

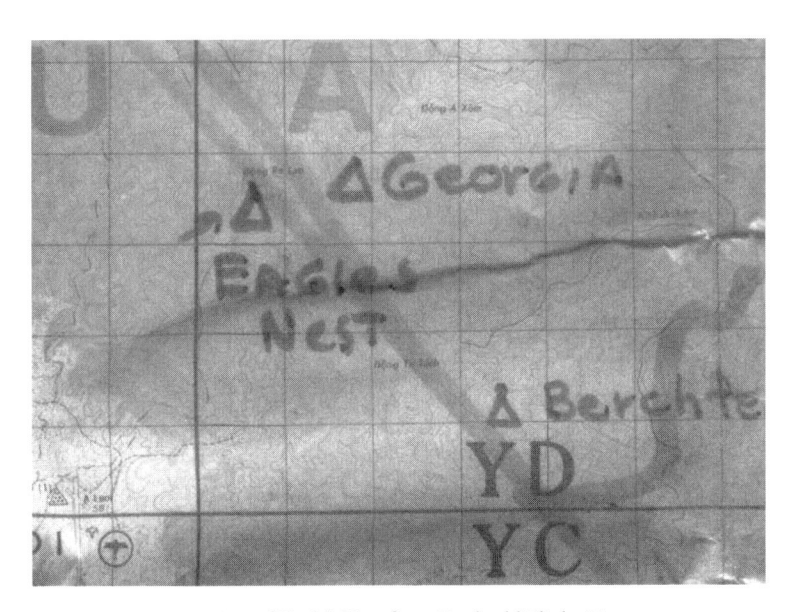

Location of Eagle's Nest from Dan's old Flight Map

An Eagle's Eye View

UH-1H/V and EH-1H/X AIRCRAFT PREVENTIVE MAINTENANCE DAILY INSPECTION CHECKLIST

GENERAL INFORMATION AND SCOPE

WARNING: certain inspections are mandatory safety-of-flight requirements, and the inspection intervals cannot be exceeded. In the event these inspections cannot be accomplished at the specified interval, the aircraft condition status symbol will be immediately changed to a red x. these type inspection items are preceded by "mandatory safety-of-flight inspection item".

Note: individual inspection items contained in this manual are considered the minimum requirements for performing a daily inspection and must be performed. The cumulative effects of inspection deferrals are unknown and could result in catastrophic failure or increased maintenance at a later date. Therefore, the use of special lettering to emphasize mandatory safety-of-flight inspection items is not to be construed as authority for deferral of other inspections.

Area No. 1: Nose Area:
all surfaces, components, and equipment in nose compartment and on exterior ahead of crew doors.

Area No. 2: Cabin Exterior and Landing Gear Left Side: all surfaces, components, and equipment on cabin exterior and underside between forward sides of crew doors and aft cabin walls. Includes landing gear, and forward fuel cell sump on cabin underside. Includes compartment in pylon island below main transmission

Area No. 3: Engine Area Left Side: all surfaces, components, and equipment associated with engine installation, located above engine work deck and within engine cowling, tailpipe fairing and intake fairing

Area No. 4: Tailboom Area: all surfaces, components, and equipment located in or on the tail boom and vertical fin. Including access compartments below engine work deck and aft of cabin walls.

Area No. 5: Engine Area Right Side: all surfaces, components, and equipment associated with engine installation, located above engine work deck and within engine cowling, tailpipe fairing and intake fairing

An Eagle's Eye View

Area No. 6: Cabin Exterior and Landing Gear Right Side:
all surfaces, components, and equipment on cabin exterior and underside between forward sides of crew doors and aft cabin walls. Includes landing gear, and forward fuel cell sump on cabin underside. Includes compartment in pylon island below main transmission

Area No. 7: Upper Pylon Area
all surfaces, components, and equipment of the main rotor pylon group, from top of mast to the bottom of th etransmision mounts. Includes main rotor, mast and rotating controls, transmission with accessories and mounts, and main input drive shaft. Includes top of cabin surface and components.

Area No. 8: Lower Pylon Area (via Cabin Interior and Interior Area)
all surfaces, components, and equipment inside of cabin area, between forward sides of crew doors and aft cabin walls and pylon area including bottom of transmission, electrical and hydraulic components.

104

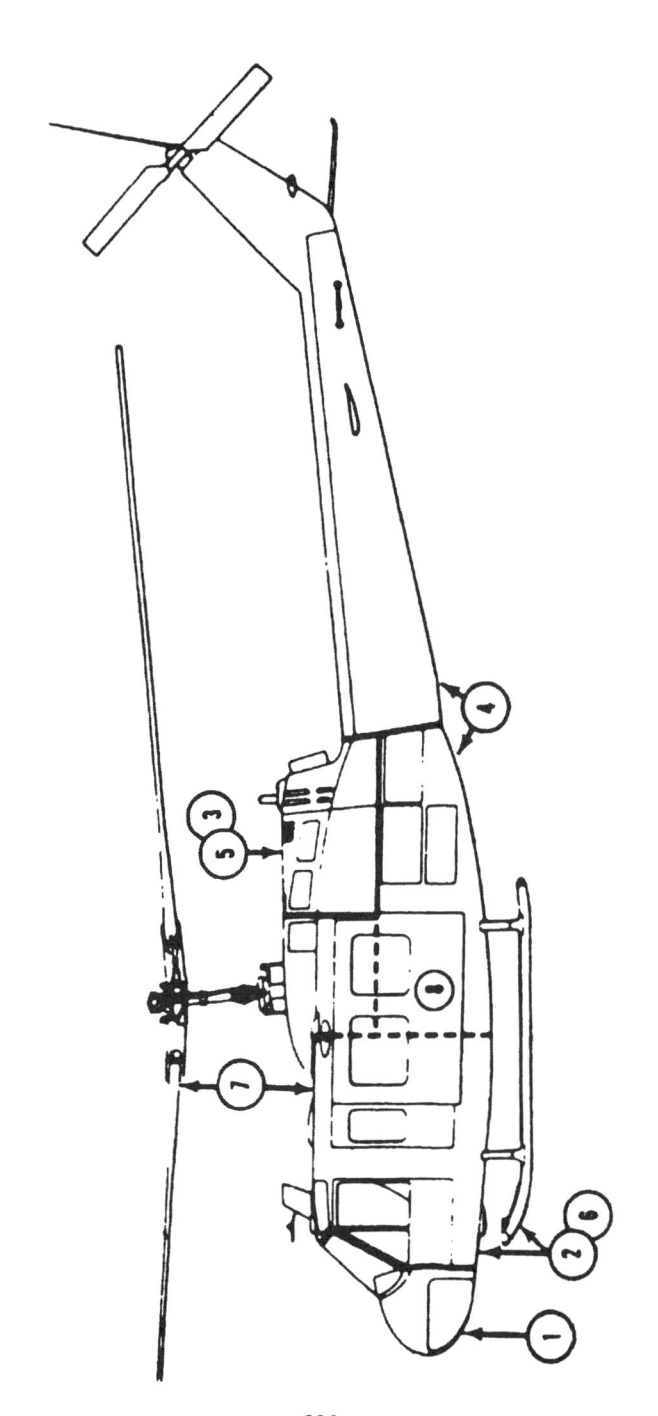

To order a copy of this book online go to:
http://www.aneagleseyeview.net/

To order by U.S.P.S:
Please send a Cashier's Check/Money Order payable to:

Terry Willman
P.O. Box 54895
Phoenix, Arizona 85078-4895

Includes Shipping Charges
$10.25 U.S.
$12.45 Canada U.S. Currency Only
$16.40 Out of U.S. & U.S. Currency Only

U.S. Please allow up to 4 weeks on delivery
Out of U.S. Please allow up to 6weeks on delivery